The AMY HIPPO Curriculum Guide

for Teachers and Counselors

and Parents too!

Mallory V. White, LPC

and Lauren Ahl

Letter from the Author

Dear fellow counselors, educators, and parents,

Thank you for your ongoing support for Amy Hippo's mission of emotional wellness and this opportunity to collaborate towards increased confidence and well-being in our children. I share these strategies in an effort to support and network with my colleagues and to help spark new energy into the powerful work you do every day. Practicing the techniques I detail in this guide has resulted in significant success both professionally, as a counselor and resource coordinator, and personally, as a parent to my children. I hope you'll find similar results should you choose to explore these ideas in your practice as professionals and parents.

For Counselors: I write to you as an LPC (Licensed Professional Counselor) specializing in CBT (Cognitive Behavioral Therapy) and TF-CBT (Trauma-Focused Cognitive Behavioral Therapy). This book provides a 12 to 16-week counseling session guide that is customizable to match your clients' individual treatment plans and goals while maintaining consistency in concepts of CBT throughout the counseling experience. I'll show you how I keep my clients excited to come back each week and tailor my services differently for varying developmental levels for clients aged 5-18.

For Educators: I write to you as a public charter school resource coordinator, and SEL (social-emotional learning) committee member. As an advocate for increased availability of SEL Programs in our school system, I provide you with a 9-week guide to classroom wellness and a road map to bringing the Amy Hippo program to your elementary students and their families. Let the growth and classroom bonding begin!

For Parents: Mom - of all the titles I've earned in my lifetime, this one is the greatest honor. My family is built on a foundation of love and grace for each of our biological, step, foster, and adopted children.

What I've learned in my profession has helped me tremendously in shaping emotionally intelligent children at home. We certainly have hard days and significant challenges in our lives, yet when my children feel anxious to try something new, they successfully talk to their own Amy Hippo and lower the intensity of anxiety's impact on their day-to-day living. When they encounter a nervous peer, they can teach their friends where fear comes from and how it helps us, hurts us, or blocks us from fully finding joy. This has been such a gift to them and their friendships, and I hope it helps your children too.

Have fun in these next chapters exploring and brainstorming ways that this might work for your roles at home and the office. I strive for the website, blogs, and feedback forms to allow us to get connected and network together to best support our communities. We are in roles as helping professionals and cultivators of resilient (and kind) humans. Trust me, these jobs are easier and more fun when we have each other to lean on.

Thank you for your commitment to your communities and your passion for supporting children. See you in the field!

Very Warmly,
Mallory V. White

Contents

Worksheets provided in this book are available as printable PDF
downloads at www.amyhippo.com

Teachers and Educators

Date	Lesson Targets	Class Activity
Week 1	**Welcome Day** – Meet Amy Hippo, overview & discussion **Read:** Amy Hippo Intro	**Create:** Color Amy Hippo worksheet
Week 2	**Discussion:** Feelings **Lesson:** Anger Iceberg	**Complete:** Anger Iceberg worksheet using a whole group example
Week 3 **<u>BADGE #1</u>**	**Read:** Amy Hippo Part 1 (Flight) **Lesson:** My 3 Zones	**Create:** Color Three Zones worksheet **Create:** Color Badge 1 & glue to Amy Hippo worksheet
Week 4	**Review:** 3 Zones & Iceberg **Read**: Amy Hippo Part 2 (Freeze)	**Complete:** Classroom list of real-life examples of flight or freeze.

Week 5 **BADGE #2**	**Read:** Amy Hippo Part 3 (Fight) **Discuss:** Make an Iceberg for Becka James **Lesson:** What are ANTs?	**Complete:** A classroom list of ANTs examples found in friends, TV characters, book characters, movies, songs **Create:** Color Badge 2 & glue to Amy Hippo worksheet
Week 6 **BADGE #3**	**Discussion:** How does it all connect? **Lesson:** ANTs Review **Seek:** Find 5 hidden illustrated ANTs in the Amy Hippo book	**Complete:** ANTs activity **Create:** Color Badge 3 & glue to Amy Hippo worksheet
Week 7	**Read:** Amy Hippo Part 4 (Coping) **Learn:** Coping Skills **Discussion:** How will you fill your toolbox?	**Complete:** Make a list of coping skills as a group **Create:** Draw a toolbox on the back of your Amy Hippo and fill it with coping skills

Week 8 **<u>BADGE #4</u>**	**Discussion:** What's in my toolbox? **Review:** Growth recap	**Reverse:** Four class volunteers to teach/recap the following: *1. Anger Iceberg,* *2. Three Zones,* *3. ANTs,* *4. Coping* **Create:** Color Badge 4 and glue to Amy Hippo worksheet
Week 9	**GRADUATION DAY!!** Let's celebrate the big achievement with a fun snack and time to share your hippos. Take a class photo holding up all the Amy Hippo drawings with their badges. Great work! You're now in charge of your Amy Hippo! She doesn't get to control you anymore.	Bring your own hippo home as a reminder that you're now powerful enough to calm Amy Hippo down anytime she tries to save you when you don't truly need her help.

Week 1
Introduction and Amy Hippo

Summary:

In week one, students are introduced to the Amy Hippo learning plan they will be covering as a class over the next nine weeks, one lesson per week. Students will be introduced to the character of Amy Hippo, as well as discuss emotions experienced in our students' everyday lives. The class will start on the curriculum reading material, the book *Amy Hippo: The Superhero Who Tried Too Hard*. At the end of the week one lesson, students will color their own Amy Hippo coloring page to use throughout the lesson plan.

Objectives:
- Introduce Amy Hippo to students
- Encourage student engagement in discussion questions
- Develop an awareness of one's emotions and behaviors
- Pique interest in learning about one's emotions
- Engage in the Amy Hippo worksheet and reading material

Time for lesson: 30 minutes

Resources and Supplies:
- *Amy Hippo: The Superhero Who Tried Too Hard* (Introduction section only and Amy Asks #1)
- Amy Hippo Worksheet (Page 98 & online as PDF)
- Coloring supplies

Lesson Plan:

Before the day of the lesson, the teacher will review the content and curriculum schedule. For the first day, the teacher will explain who Amy Hippo is and what the next nine weeks of the curriculum entail. It's an exciting two months of learning about emotions and how to manage them, filled with reading, activities, earning badges, and a graduation celebration to end it all. To start, students must be introduced to a new superhero, Amy Hippo.

Amy Hippo is a character in the book the class will be reading and discussing these next couple of weeks. Her character in the book is an emotional superhero who is diligently trying to protect her best friend, Becka James, by saving her from difficult moments of anxiety and panic. Yet, Amy Hippo is an untrained superhero whose efforts to help her best friend only lead to more chaotic and explosive events for Becka. Amy Hippo and Becka must learn to work together and find positive emotional skills to help handle strong and overwhelming emotions. In fact, Amy Hippo's name is even short for the parts of our brain responsible for responses of fear and anxiety, the Amygdala and Hippocampus. Having met Amy Hippo, the teacher can start approaching the goal of the curriculum – to learn about big emotions and develop healthy coping skills to manage them, alongside creating a personal Amy Hippo to go on this journey with each student. But what are big emotions?

Big emotions are ones that feel overwhelming and uncontrollable, they seem to make situations in life harder and more difficult to process. In other words, feelings that don't make us feel too good about ourselves and our lives. These are emotions we all experience at some point in our everyday lives such as anxiety, panic, fear, worry, and stress. However, through learning about Amy Hippo and ways to navigate these big emotions, one can learn to understand and cope with these feelings so they don't control us anymore.

From here, the teacher will introduce *Amy Hippo: The Superhero Who Tried Too Hard* to students, reading the introduction section together. In the introduction, students will find a note from Amy Hippo welcoming her new friends and discussing what the rest of the book has in store for them. This book will focus on Becka and Amy Hippo's journey through difficult moments of anxiety, panic, fear, anger, and self-doubt with discussion questions at each stopping point throughout the book. Following the introduction letter, the class will find the first Amy Asks questions to answer and discuss as a group.

The teacher can encourage participation amongst the classroom using the guided question prompts to facilitate discussion on emotions and student experiences. These questions can open the door to increasing effective communication skills and development of emotional awareness. Students can acknowledge first-hand what these emotions feel like, as well as support and empathize with their peers.

Throughout the discussion, it is important to foster a space of compassion, respect, and safety for your students. Students should feel comfortable sharing with their peers, as well as exploring what these emotions personally represent. After going through the discussion questions, the teacher can transition to the worksheet, an Amy Hippo coloring sheet for each student to color a personal Amy Hippo to keep throughout the rest of the lesson plan. Students can color and decorate their Amy Hippo to their liking as they will continue to add to the worksheet as the weeks progress. This will be the student's own emotional superhero to keep and learn through each lesson, as well as graduate with the student at the end of the curriculum. This activity provides a concrete guide for students to visualize this superhero helping them in their lives. After the teacher's allocated time to work on the Amy Hippo worksheet, have the students write their name on their worksheet to either collect or have them hold onto until next week's lesson.

Conclusion:

At the end of the lesson, students will develop an understanding of Amy Hippo and an awareness of what big emotions are. Students will also have colored and completed an Amy Hippo to keep and use throughout the rest of the curriculum. Throughout the rest of the week, the teacher can incorporate conversations on emotions through other lessons and readings to further the students' awareness of emotions. This lesson will prepare the students for the following weeks in exploring what emotions are and how to manage them with more fun worksheets, lessons, and badge achievements.

Review:
- Introduce lesson plan, reading material, and Amy Hippo to students
- Discuss what big emotions are with students
- Read introduction and complete discussion questions as a class
- Color Amy Hippo worksheet

Modifications and Options:

Each teacher is different, and this curriculum can be adapted to fit each teacher's classroom. Some examples include the reading and discussion questions, students can work as a class or work in groups to read and work on the discussion.

Other modifications include the coloring of the Amy Hippo worksheet. If a teacher has the resources, students can make their Amy Hippo out of felt or decorate it with different crafting materials. If printing Amy Hippo worksheets for each student is not feasible, students can draw their own Amy Hippos to color and keep. The time for each lesson can be modified for each classroom whether the discussion takes longer or more time is allowed for the creation of Amy Hippo.

Week 2
Big Emotions and Anger Iceberg

Summary:

In week two, the teacher will discuss big emotions with the class, posing questions regarding what these big feelings are, what they feel like, when they occur, and what we can all do to manage them. After this discussion, students will be introduced to the Anger Iceberg, completing a worksheet on the topic after the lesson.

Objectives:
- Students discuss what big emotions mean and analyze moments where they might have felt these emotions, particularly anger
- Develop increased communication skills to voice feelings behind expressions of anger
- Demonstrate an understanding of the Anger Iceberg (Anger is a secondary emotion with vulnerable emotions hidden underneath that project outwardly to others as anger)
- Draw conclusions from relationships between displayed emotions and hidden emotions
- Analyze what these outward emotions mean and what primary emotions are being felt beneath the surface
- Participate in discussion and complete worksheet

Time for lesson: 30 minutes

Resources and Supplies:
- Anger Iceberg worksheet (page 101 & online as PDF download)

Lesson Plan:

Before the lesson, the teacher will review the Anger Iceberg content and prepare the Anger Iceberg worksheet for students. To start the lesson, the teacher will refresh students on what big emotions are, giving and asking for examples of big emotions and moments where these emotions took control. The teacher can discuss feelings of anxiety, panic, fear, or anger that are brought on by different situations in one's life. These big emotions are normal to experience but can often feel uncomfortable, scary, or overwhelming. There are many situations where one could face these overwhelming feelings – while taking a test, after losing an important item, or having to perform in front of a crowd. These situations can have one feel strong emotions that seem to make some situations harder to manage.

Although these emotions can feel uncontrollable or confusing, there is a reason for every emotion we feel. At times we may not be initially aware of why we feel this way or even understand what these emotions might mean. With taking a test, we might feel scared or anxious. But why? Perhaps we are worried about failing or letting our parents down. The teacher can use other examples, asking the class why one might feel a big emotion in that moment. From here, the teacher can transition into the Anger Iceberg lesson.

With these big emotions, there is often more lying underneath the surface. Here the teacher can create a visual for the classroom on the board. Consider the iceberg in our oceans, we can see a small tip of ice above the surface of the water, but underneath the water is the biggest part of the iceberg, a much larger piece of ice compared to what we see above the water. The tip of the iceberg represents anger that is observable to others around us. In the world of mental health care, anger is often referred to as a "secondary emotion." In our Western society, anger is seen as commonplace and not often associated with weakness or vulnerability, therefore, it can feel fairly safe for us to display our anger outwardly. That anger is often fueled by primary emotions that frequently provoke sensations of vulnerability when expressed. Hence, primary feelings of shame or fear may be expressed with the secondary response of anger as a defense against vulnerability.

For example, you did something embarrassing at school and everyone laughed. Your first reaction visible to others might be anger, but inside you feel embarrassed, ashamed, worthless, or sad. You might not understand why you feel this way or don't want to show that to your friends and peers since allowing increased vulnerability in a public setting can feel intimidating and scary in itself. Instead, you immediately react with anger, allowing that secondary emotional response. Place the word "anger" at the tip of the iceberg and "embarrassed," "ashamed," "worthless," and "sad" in the hidden ice below the surface. This creates a concrete visualization of our experience with anger. Once our experience with anger is expressed as an Anger Iceberg worksheet then we can work to increase our effective communication skills. Teachers will now have a new vocabulary to check on their students throughout the school year by suggesting in moments of conflict, "Let's see what could be happening with your Anger Iceberg." and working with the student to better verbalize their experience with anger.

To further the class's understanding, you can pose more examples of situations where one might be expressing anger and dismissing what they might be feeling under the surface. Continue with additional examples on the board, visually showing the different emotions that lie under the surface. Write the word "anger" at the tip of the iceberg and allow the class to suggest examples of the hidden primary emotions that may be fueling that expression of anger for each example scenario. The Anger Iceberg is a way to dig deeper into one's emotions and understand what they are feeling to better manage these feelings in the future. Understanding these emotions can be empowering and help minimize anger outbursts. Ultimately, if we learn to verbally express the feelings underneath anger without escalating to outward displays of anger then we've just achieved healthy communication, strong emotional intelligence, and increased self-control.

After the lesson, the teacher can pass out the Anger Iceberg worksheets to complete individually or as a group, discussing responses as an option afterward. This worksheet can be used throughout the school year to support effective interpersonal communication and conflict resolution skills among classmates. Place the iceberg worksheet with the Amy Hippo coloring page at the end of the lesson.

Conclusion:

After the lesson, students will have a sufficient understanding of the Anger Iceberg as well as expand their emotional vocabulary and communication skills. Students will be prepared to discuss emotions more readily and recount what an Anger Iceberg is going into next week. They will also be able to recognize more examples from their lives of primary emotions and secondary responses.

Review:

- Review and discuss anger – what is it, how do we show it, why is it there
- Discuss what situations might result in feelings of anger
- Introduce the Anger Iceberg and work with examples of what emotions lie under the surface of an anger response
- Work on Anger Iceberg worksheet and practice communicating the primary emotions behind the secondary emotion of anger.

Modifications and Options:

With this lesson, there are different ways to approach the material for different teaching styles and classrooms. Visuals can help better explain the concept of big emotions and the Anger Iceberg, as well as encourage participation. Students can have written examples of triggers for anger as a writing or presentation assignment.

The discussion and worksheet can be completed in groups, individually, or with the class. If printing the worksheet is not feasible, students can create their own iceberg to fill in and complete. Students can also explore the article on Anger Icebergs on the Amy Hippo website to learn and answer discussion or text-based analysis questions based on the article.

Week 3
Anger Iceberg Badge and Three Zones

Summary:

In week three, the teacher will review last week's lesson on Anger Icebergs, with the class. Showcasing an understanding of the concept, students will be awarded their first badge, the Anger Iceberg badge. Students will celebrate their accomplishment by coloring, cutting out, and affixing the badge to their Amy Hippo coloring page from week one. The class will go on to read "Part One: Flight" and discuss "Amy Hippo Asks #2" questions. After the reading, the teacher will explain the next lesson on the Three Zones to students and have the class complete a worksheet on the topic.

Objectives:

- Demonstrate an understanding of the prior lesson on Anger Icebergs
- Engage with reading material and analyze the main character's conflict and reaction within the story
- Participate in group discussion, responding and expressing thoughts on their experiences with emotions
- Show understanding of Three Zones lesson, comparing the different zones and explaining their meaning and effects
- Complete Three Zones worksheet individually with comprehension of the topic

Time for lesson: 30 minutes

Resources and Supplies:

- *Amy Hippo: The Superhero Who Tried Too Hard* (Part 1: Flight and Amy Asks #2)
- Three Zones worksheet (page 102 & online as PDF)
- Badges coloring page (page 99 & online as PDF)
- Amy Hippo worksheet from Week One
- Coloring supplies
- Scissors
- Glue

Lesson Plan:

Before the lesson, teachers will familiarize themselves with the Three Zones concept and prepare the worksheet with coloring pages for the class. To start the lesson, teachers will review the Anger Iceberg lesson from last week with students to test their retention of the topic. Questions to pose could include:

- What does the Anger Iceberg represent?
- What tough secondary emotion do we generally feel safe showing others?
- What types of emotions hide below the surface that can result in expressions of anger?
- Why don't we feel as comfortable expressing those feelings outwardly?
- What are ways to better understand and express our emotions?

After demonstrating proficiency on the topic, the teacher will congratulate the class and award them their first badge, the Anger Iceberg badge. The class can celebrate their achievement in earning this new skill and mastering the concept. Celebrating the badge is an important milestone and encourages and excites the students to keep working towards the remaining badges. Students will receive their badge to color, cut out, and affix to their Amy Hippo. The teacher has the option to color and apply the badges at the end of the lesson to ensure enough time for the content or to work on them before moving on with the rest of the lesson.

After receiving their new badge, the class will move on to reading "Part One: Flight" as a group. In the story, students will meet the main character, Becka James, and her superhero, Amy Hippo, though the two aren't the best at working together. They will follow Becka to her first class where she experiences the first big emotional hardship of the book. Becka experiences anxiety that escalates to panic after being called to the front of the class to solve a problem on the board. As Becka's anxiety and panic increases in front of her classmates, Amy Hippo swoops in, pulling Becka out of the situation and sending her fleeing out of the classroom.

The teacher can ask students what they believe happened to Becka when she cried in front of the class and ran out of the room. Why do they think Amy Hippo was pulling Becka out of the classroom? After receiving the student's perspective on the story, the class can move on to answering Amy Hippo's discussion questions on the next page. Students can approach the questions by sharing stories of feeling embarrassed or scared, as well as their experiences of being nervous or worried in a school setting.

After facilitating a group discussion on emotions and students' own experiences, the teacher can introduce the last lesson of the day, the Three Zones lesson. The teacher can have students imagine a bullseye or draw one on the board to visualize and signify each zone. The Three Zones symbolize the three stages of emotional experiences we find ourselves in across varying situations. The first zone, right in the middle of the target, is the **Comfort and Safety Zone** – a zone where we feel comfortable and most at ease, like at home with our feet up or reading in the park. We can relax and recharge in this zone because nothing is challenging or pushing us and we are safe here. This zone is important to help us relax and recharge daily while giving us time to release tensions and let our guard down. Though this stage sounds nice and easy, we are not growing in this zone, so it's important to routinely move beyond the Comfort and Safety Zone. It's also vital that we return to this zone to unwind and embrace feeling secure in our space.

In the next zone, we are moved to a less comfortable space filled with possibilities for progress and discovery. The **Growth and Learning Zone** is the zone where one is ready to engage and be focused on new situations and ideas. Whether in school or social situations, this stage encourages being present and willing to act and interact. This is a stage of personal growth and new experiences where we could feel anxious in these moments, especially as we're faced with unfamiliar things. However, these feelings of anxiety and tension are normal and healthy to have. It's natural to feel a bit of anxiety and nerves going into a new situation, but these uncertain feelings will eventually subside the more you do it and allow you to grow through difficult moments with more ease in the future. Yet, in the final zone, the final ring of the target, those early feelings of anxiety and worry reach an intense level and hinder one's progress. This zone, the **Fear and Anger Zone**, affects the logical side of your brain, turning off rational thought and increasing reliance on emotional responses.

14

It's easy to cross into the Fear and Anger Zone when you respond only from your emotional side – similar to the Anger Iceberg, only responding with anger without considering everything else going on. This is where Amy Hippo swoops in – the emotional side of your brain is the Amy Hippo control center. From here, Amy Hippo (your brain's **amy**gdala and **hippo**campus) only allows you to react with fight, flight or freeze. In these moments, it's important to find ways to move back to the middle zone to continue one's growth and positive handling of new situations. This will become achievable with the aid of personal coping skills taught in the upcoming weeks of this course.

With this new concept, the teacher can refer to the book, quizzing students on what zone Becka is in throughout "Part One" and how she responded when facing these zones. After discussing more about the zones and the story, the teacher can transition the class to their last assignment for the lesson, the Three Zones worksheet. To complete the worksheet, instruct students to color each zone a different color and write one example of an experience in each zone. For example, color the Comfort and Safety Zone green and write "napping" or "movie night" in the center zone. Next, color the Learning and Growth Zone yellow and write "school" or "soccer practice" as the experience. Then, color the Fear and Panic Zone red and write a possible example of "riding a new rollercoaster" or "getting in trouble". Last, instruct the students to draw their own facial expressions in the boxes below from the examples they provided for each zone. This will allow them to see how their body and facial expressions change as they move into different zones.

After completion of the Three Zones worksheet the class can move on to color their new Anger Iceberg badge and glue it to their Amy Hippo worksheet from Week One. More badges will be added, so ensure students have enough space to add more.

Conclusion:

After the lesson, students will be motivated from earning their first badge to continue the lessons with excitement each week. The class will demonstrate an understanding of their curriculum reading material to further read and analyze in the coming weeks. They will continue to develop an awareness and comfortability by participating in discussions and sharing their experiences with emotions.

Going into the next week, students will have the ability to recognize the Three Zones through examples in their other subjects, such as characters in literature, as well as recall the Three Zones to review in the next lesson. At the end of the week, students will have a greater understanding of their emotions and the different layers of how they react and respond to certain situations.

Review:
- Review the Anger Iceberg lesson
- Celebrate the first badge – The Anger Iceberg badge
- Read "Part One: Flight" and answer discussion questions
- Learn about the Three Zones and complete Three Zones worksheet
- Color, cut, and glue the badge to the Amy Hippo coloring page

Modifications and Options:

In this lesson, the teacher can modify the review process to fit the classroom. This can occur by forming questions and having students raise their hands, having the class respond in a group setting, or having a small written assignment for students to work on giving answers in their own words.

As for the badges, the celebration or coloring can be held for the beginning or end of the lesson. The teacher can also bring something in or create a display to celebrate the students' achievement, such as playing music for students to dance to or bringing in a small surprise like a snack or a drink for students to enjoy as they color their badge. For the badges, students can color each badge one by one with each lesson, then cut and glue them after the last one is earned and colored as a class activity.

With the Three Zones lesson, the teacher can use the concept in other lesson areas by having students analyze what zone a character in their English assignment is in to further demonstrate an understanding and proficiency on the topic. This lesson can be modified to fit the structure of the classroom and classroom schedule to best suit the teacher and students.

Week 4
Amy Hippo and Fight, Flight, or Freeze

Summary:

In this lesson, the teacher will review the Three Zones and the Anger Iceberg lessons with students. After the review, the class will go on to read "Part Two: Freeze" from the curriculum reading material and address the discussion questions after the story. The teacher will work with the class to make a list of triggering events that would cause one to flee (similar to the prior chapter) or freeze (as experienced in the current chapter).

Objectives:
- Students demonstrate a proficient understanding of the Three Zones and Anger Iceberg
- Analyze situations about big emotions and determine what emotions are being felt under the surface and what zone is present
- Participate in discussion after finishing the reading material
- Discuss events of the story and form opinions on the situations the main character faces
- Express experiences of triggering events and build on the ideas of other students
- Identify triggering situations where one might flee or freeze

Time for lesson: 30 minutes

Resources and Supplies:
- *Amy Hippo: The Superhero Who Tried Too Hard*, "Part Two: Freeze" and "Amy Asks #3"
- Amy Hippo worksheet – from Week One

Lesson Plan:

In this week's lesson, the class will review the Anger Iceberg and Three Zones with questions on the concept and examples for students to practice. Students will also be asked for examples of how one can address anxiety and panic, as well as how to move from the Fear and Anger Zone back into the Growth and Learning Zone. These examples will help facilitate a deeper understanding of emotions while showcasing analytical and problem-solving skills.

After the review, the class will move on to the reading material for the week, "Part Two: Freeze". In this section, Becka James, is assigned to be the goalie for her team's first soccer game. Her nerves and daydreaming get the best of her and she misses the ball, allowing the other team to score a point. Becka begins to panic, similar to how she felt in the first story, and Amy Hippo swoops in to help her. However, Amy Hippo's help causes Becka to freeze, missing the next goal completely. At the end of the story, Becka is upset, feeling like she let her team down and experiences self-doubt.

After finishing the story, the teacher will ask students what happened to Becka in the story, why she froze, and what might have caused her to freeze. The class can move on to the discussion questions, asking for students' opinions on how they would have helped Becka and what they would have done if they were in Becka's shoes. Students can analyze the situations in the story and their own experiences to add to the discussion.

After the discussion, the teacher will make a list of triggering events and situations where one might run away or freeze in response to overwhelming situations. Examples can include: performing in front of a large crowd, having to confess to something, or facing an embarrassing moment. Students can be encouraged to share their stories where they froze or ran away or moments they pushed through those feelings.

Conclusion:

At the end of the lesson, students will have an understanding of the Anger Iceberg and Three Zones with a better grasp of what these emotions mean and how to recognize them. The class will move forward with the reading material, adding more to the discussion and demonstrating an awareness of the situations the main character faces in the story.

By recognizing the events of the story, students will have increased opportunities for practice in recognizing situations where characters, people in their lives, or themselves are facing situations that have placed them within the worrisome Fear and Anger Zone.

Review:

- Review Anger Iceberg and Three Zones lessons with examples to analyze and discuss
- Read "Part Two: Freeze" and answer discussion questions as a class
- Have students help make a list of examples of possible triggering events that could result in flight or freeze responses

Modifications and Options:

In this lesson, teachers can approach the review in a way that works best for their students, such as asking questions around the room, working in groups, or having a game-like review session. The goal is for students to show proficiency in the concept. Teachers can also use examples from other class readings for students to analyze and further relate to the content.

With the discussion questions after "Part Two: Freeze", students can work on these questions as a class, a group, or individually by written response. With the list of triggering events, students can add suggestions on how to handle certain situations, what they might do to calm down, or how they would address their feelings in the moment.

Week 5
Three Zones Badge and ANTs

Summary:

This week, the teacher will review the Three Zones, with students earning and celebrating their third badge, the Three Zones badge, to color and affix to their Amy Hippo at the end of the lesson. The class will read the third story of the book, "Part Three: Fight", and discuss the different reasons why Becka reacted the way she did in the story. Students will go on to create an Anger Iceberg for Becka to consider what she was feeling underneath her anger response. Afterwards, the teacher will introduce the concept for this week's lesson, ANTs or Automatic Negative Thoughts. Students will complete an activity listing ANTs they have experienced or have seen in other forms of media. The lesson will end with students coloring and gluing their badge to their Amy Hippo.

Objectives:
- Demonstrate proficiency in the Three Zones review
- Discuss the text and form opinions based on their observations of what the character is feeling and how they reacted
- Use their understanding of the Anger Iceberg to create one for the character in the story
- Analyze the actions of the character to form an observation of the other emotions she might be feeling and the reasons why she reacted with anger instead
- Discuss their new lesson on ANTs, providing examples from their lives or media

Time for Lesson: 30-45 minutes

Resources and Supplies:
- *Amy Hippo: The Superhero Who Tried Too Hard* (Part 3: Fight and Amy Asks #4)
- Anger Iceberg worksheet (page 101 & online PDF)
- ANTs cards and blog (page 103, to be used with online blog)
- Badges coloring page from Week Three

- Amy Hippo worksheet from Week One
- Coloring supplies
- Scissors
- Glue

Lesson Plan:

In this lesson, students will review the Three Zones, proving their knowledge of the concept. With questions to consider:

· What are the names and placement of each zone?

· What does each zone mean?

· Why do we move between zones?

· What can someone do to move from the Fear and Anger Zone to the Growth and Learning zone?

· Provide examples of characters in media or literature. Have students determine what zone the character is in, and if in the fear and anger zone, what the character can do to move out of that zone.

After the questions, the teacher will award the students their third badge, the Three Zones badge. The classroom will celebrate their achievement, coloring and gluing their badges to their Amy Hippo at the end of the lesson.

The class will continue on by reading "Part Three: Fight". This story follows Becka, right after the soccer game from the previous lesson, sitting with her family at dinner. Becka is riddled with negative thoughts and self-doubt from her emotional day, with her anger getting the best of her. Distracted, she misses her grandparents talking to her, causing Becka to be scolded by her mom for ignoring her grandparents. Noticing that Becka is feeling a rush of anxiety and panic, Amy Hippo swoops in to help her best friend. With Amy's help, Becka slams down her fists flinging spaghetti across the table and exclaiming in anger. A defeated Becka is sent to her room where she cries herself to sleep.

In the story, Becka was overwhelmed by all the feelings and thoughts going on in her body, leading her to impulsively react with anger and frustration. However, this only caused her to feel worse as she made a mess at the dinner table and upset her parents. Speaking with the class, the teacher can ask students what happened in this moment for Becka to react that way. Going into the discussion questions, students will be asked to point out why Becka reacted the way she did and how they would change the story to help Becka in this situation. Students can use examples from their lives where anger and negative thoughts got in the way and affected how they reacted.

After the discussion, students will be asked to create an Anger Iceberg for Becka based on the situation they read about in the story. Becka showed anger by yelling and banging her fists on the table, but what was she really feeling underneath the anger that she didn't communicate? Students can work as a class, in multiple groups, or individually on the Anger Iceberg assignment to discuss afterward.

Once Becka's iceberg assignment is completed, the class can move on to the next lesson and activity regarding ANTs. ANTs stands for Automatic Negative Thoughts, and these are thoughts that pop into our heads that hold a rather negative perspective of ourselves, the world, and the future situations we face that are not based on truth or solid evidence. Automatic Negative Thoughts are completely normal responses to have and something we all face. Our mind generates these thoughts effortlessly, but all it wants to do is protect us from issues and possible threats. Sometimes our negative thoughts are a habit we have formed over the years. However, our negative thoughts can grow and get in the way, creating more hardships in our daily lives that can impact our mental health.

These ANTs (Automatic Negative Thoughts) are named after ants because thoughts can pop up and ruin your day – similar to a picnic with ants getting all over the food – and with one ant, there are plenty more to follow if we let it get out of control. However, being aware of these Automatic Negative Thought patterns can be beneficial in recognizing why these thoughts are present, if they are important, and real or not. The teacher can list several types of ANTs people commonly face, asking students to give examples of negative thoughts for each type. With these examples, the class can make a list of ANTs they might have experienced first-hand or observed in media. The ANTs blog at www.amyhippo.com lists and defines nine of the most commonly experienced ANTs and shares additional resources on negative thinking patterns.

After discussing the examples of ANTs, students can move on to coloring their newly awarded badge to cut and add to their Amy

Hippo at the end of the lesson. The Amy Hippos will then be collected or put away once everyone is finished.

Conclusion:

At the end of the lesson, students will have demonstrated an understanding of the Three Zones, earning their second badge to add to their Amy Hippo. The students will have a better grasp on analyzing big emotions and the reasons one might react with emotion rather than logic. Students will have an idea of what ANTs are with examples to consider prior to earning their next badge, the ANTs badge.

Review:

- Review Three Zones, rewarding the class with the third badge, the Three Zones badge
- Read "Part Three: Fight" and answer discussion questions
- Create an Anger Iceberg for Becka James based on the reading
- Introduce ANTs and create a list of different ANTs
- Color, cut, and glue the third badge to Amy Hippo

Modifications and Options:

With this lesson, students have two activities that can be completed as a class, small groups, or individually. Discussing the book and Becka's reaction, students can act out the situation exploring different ways Becka or the other people in the scene could have responded to the situation.

Earning badges is always a celebration. The teacher can consider creating a reward or celebratory environment in these moments. Rewards could include extra recess time, a piece of candy or a snack, or a no homework day. As for the environment, the teacher can play music while students color their badges or work on their activities.

Week 6
ANTs Review and Badge

Summary:

In week six, the class will review ANTs and discuss how all the elements learned so far connect. Students will work on finding five ANTs in the book, discussing how ANTs affect our mood and then celebrating and coloring the newly earned ANTs badge to cut and glue to their Amy Hippo.

Objectives:
- Express an understanding of ANTs, analyzing and pointing out ANTs within the text
- Identify how ANTs affect one's mood and actions

Time for Lesson: 30-45 minutes

Resources and Supplies:
- *Amy Hippo: The Superhero Who Tried Too Hard*
- Notebook paper
- Badges coloring page from Week Three
- Amy Hippo worksheet from Week One
- Coloring supplies
- Scissors
- Glue

Lesson Plan:

In this lesson, students will review the three concepts they have learned so far (Anger Icebergs, Three Zones, and ANTs) to showcase their mastery of these topics. This review will lead to a discussion on how it all connects.
- What do each of these lessons mean and how do they come together in the book and our everyday life?
- How can we compare each lesson and discuss their impact and benefits?

The three concepts are all means of exploring one's emotions and the different forms and expressions they take. Each concept considers looking at situations and handling emotions with a certain rationale and awareness, or, in other situations, with an emotionally driven response. Each part of our brain must be on to handle the situations around us and our emotional responses to them. When our emotions take control and get in the way of our ability to process situations, we start to face levels of discomfort, anxiety, or fear.

For Becka James, she is repeatedly facing moments of panic and fleeing, fighting, or freezing in situations of heightened anxiety. All her emotions and ways to handle them are out of whack. Becka is unable to effectively process her emotions, burying them and reacting with anger instead. She finds herself falling into the Fear and Panic Zone and stuck in a pattern of Automatic Negative Thoughts (ANTs).

Each concept learned so far can help one become more aware of what they are feeling and how they're reacting. Thus, increasing overall emotional intelligence. Eventually, with enough consistency and care, one can keep a balance with their emotions and become prepared for any situation that comes afterward.

After the discussion, the teacher will divide the class into groups with three activities to complete and rotate through until each group completes each activity.

- <u>Activity one</u> - discussing ANTs and how they change one's mood and actions
- <u>Activity two</u> – using the book, *Amy Hippo: The Superhero Who Tried Too Hard* to find five of the ANTs expressed in the book, listing the ones they find and the corresponding ANT category (hint: look for the illustrated insect ants hidden on pages when ANTs are spoken by Becka James)
- <u>Activity three</u> – each student coloring the third badge, the ANTs badge.

Before starting the activities, the teacher will run through a short review of ANTs – quizzing students on the meaning, examples, and types - awarding the class their third badge, the ANTs badge. Once the class finishes each activity, students will share their answers for the discussion and point out the ANTs they found.

ANTs can change someone's mood by causing one to doubt and become unsure of themselves. It can keep us down with negative thoughts that hinder our everyday lives if not addressed. ANTs affect our actions by causing us to avoid the things we enjoy out of fear or act in a state of worry, hyper-focused on what we are doing wrong or who might be thinking the same thing. It can bring our emotions down causing one to react out of annoyance, frustration, or anger, as well as feeling anxious, depressed, or hopeless.

In the book, Becka has ANTs throughout the story:
- Page 12 - "...Becka knows that Amy is ruining her life…"
- Page 14 - "Amy Hippo is the worst superhero in the entire galaxy"
- Page 25 - "Amy Hippo is the worst superhero ever!"
- Page 47 - "I let everyone down."
- Page 53 - "...felt like proof that she was the worst soccer player ever."
- Page 55 - "Amy Hippo ruins everything!"
- Page 65, 66, and 67

The lesson will end with each student cutting out their badge and gluing it to their Amy Hippo.

Conclusion:

At the end of the lesson, students will demonstrate proficiency on the meaning and connection of each lesson learned, developing the ability to look through the emotions we feel and the negative thoughts we think to understand what they mean. The class will develop comfort in talking about these feelings and thoughts within class discussions to better understand what these situations mean and how to sensibly approach them. Students will feel encouraged by all the concepts they are learning and the skills they are mastering to use in their lives and share with others.

Review:
- Discuss the connection of each concept learned
- Review ANTs, discussing case examples

- Award and celebrate students with their third badge, the ANTs badge to cut and affix to the Amy Hippo worksheet
- Students work in stations discussing how ANTs affect one's mood and actions, finding five ANTs within the book, and coloring their ANTs badge
- Discuss answers from the activities as a class

Modifications and Options:

Depending on the size and resources, the activity swap can be organized to better suit the class. There can be more or fewer groups, or the activities can be completed as a class. If you have more than one copy of the book, multiple groups can work on finding the ANTs. Finding the ANTs can be done as a class with the teacher writing the quotes on the board for students to point out where each ANT can be found and it's corresponding category. The activities can be completed together, or mixed and matched with some being completed in groups. Activities can be completed similarly to the other lessons by doing the discussion, then the activity, and finishing the day with coloring, cutting, and gluing the new badge. The ways to complete this lesson are up to the teacher to best fit their classroom.

Week 7
Coping Skills and Toolbox

Summary:

    In week seven's lesson, the class will read the final section in the curriculum reading material, "Part Four: Superhero's Toolbox". Students will discuss coping skills with questions from the last discussion section of the book. Continuing with the themes of the discussion, the class will continue to talk about coping skills, creating a list of these skills as a group. Students will move on to drawing a toolbox on the back of their Amy Hippo, filling the box with coping skills that personally work for them or might help in future instances.

Objectives:
- Analyze the meaning and purpose of Amy Hippo in the story
- Compare and contrast Becka's journey from the beginning of the book to the end
- Identify what coping skills are and how they can benefit in overwhelming situations
- Participate in the discussion, building on the ideas of others and contributing to the list of coping skills
- Develop a personal list of coping skills to keep in one's toolbox

Time for lesson: 30-45 minutes

Resources and Supplies:
- *Amy Hippo: The Superhero Who Tried Too Hard* (Part 4: Superhero's Toolbox and Amy Asks #5)
- Coping skills review material (online blog)
- Amy Hippo worksheet from Week One
- Coloring supplies

Lesson Plan:

    In this week's lesson, the class will finish the reading material by completing "Part Four: Superhero's Toolbox". In this story, Becka finally learns the meaning and purpose of Amy Hippo. After multiple instances of believing Amy Hippo was just trying to make her life harder, Becka realizes that Amy Hippo was trying to help her in the moments she felt overwhelmed. Amy Hippo reads Becka's body signals, ones sent to her brain when she experiences big emotions or feelings that she's perceiving as dangerous. This causes Amy Hippo to swoop in like a superhero and help in those situations, even if Becka's not actually in real danger.

When facing anxiety or panic, we send signals of present danger to our brain and one's body naturally reacts with fight, flight, or freeze responses. However, by learning to recognize the physiological signals we are each sending to our brain, one can begin interrupting these responses with effective coping skills to calm down the emotions and relax the body, thus, reinforcing that we are safe. Coping skills are actions one can take to help reset their brain and calm down their body to better address these feelings in a more rational mind space. They can be simple activities such as drawing or playing a game, or perhaps more involved such as writing down the emotions one is feeling or by meditating. Coping skills can be momentary breaks or a time to address what one is feeling in a composed way.

Becka also realizes she is not the only one with an Amy Hippo looking out for her. Everyone has a little superhero, saving them from real dangers and helping them through their big emotions and reactions of anxiety and panic. Becka decides to sign up for classes where Amy Hippo and she can learn coping skills and techniques to send better signals to her brain, as well as for the two to work better together when things get a little tough. In the end, Becka can handle stressful situations with a bit more ease, and Amy Hippo can cheer her on along the way.

After the reading, the class will move on to the discussion questions. Students will be asked to list coping skills, as well as point out the difference between healthy and unhealthy coping skills. Healthy coping skills create long-lasting outcomes that are positive to our lives, such as reaching out to talk about one's emotions or exercising and eating healthy. These are beneficial actions that are helpful to turn to throughout one's life. As for unhealthy coping skills, these skills might feel good at first but can lead to dangerous habits with negative consequences in the future, such as over-eating, avoiding one's feelings, or withdrawing oneself from their responsibilities. These strategies could create a negative reliance and avoidance in the future, as well as make someone's feelings worse and even more stressful. Students will also discuss how they feel about Amy Hippo after learning why we all have one. Do they have a different opinion about Amy knowing she is just trying to help or annoyed that she gets in the way sometimes? This question will allow students to consider the Amy Hippo in their lives and if working with her will help their relationship in the future.

After the discussion, the teacher can prompt students to help create a list of coping skills that would help calm down big emotions. Students can pull examples from their lives or suggest new ideas. Coping skills can range from listening to music and going for a walk to dancing with family members or friends and playing with slime. Students can list an array of activities that might help, as many as they can think of – this can show students that options for coping skills are vast and different for each person – the importance is finding ones that work best for the person.

After completing a solid list of skills to refer to, students will retrieve their Amy Hippo worksheet and draw their toolbox on the back of it. This toolbox is designed by the students and is where they will write in coping skills that might help them in future situations. This will be a place for students to refer to when they are feeling overwhelming emotions and are in need of a coping skill. After the class finishes their toolbox, students can put away or collect their Amy Hippos.

Conclusion:

At the end of the lesson, students will have completed the curriculum reading with a more concise understanding of Amy Hippo and how she supports our daily lives. The class will have a personal list of coping skills to refer to and rely on when facing difficult situations in the future. Drawing near the end of the curriculum, students will have a more concise comprehension and appreciation of their emotions, the ways their bodies respond to situations, and the methods to recognize and calm these emotions.

Reviews:
- Read "Part Four: Superhero's Toolbox"
- Use questions from the discussion to talk about coping skills and Amy Hippo's purpose
- Create a large list of coping skills as a class

- Have students draw a toolbox on the back of their Amy Hippo and fill the box with coping skills they can use when needed

Modifications and Options:

With the coping skills activity, teachers can put students in groups to see how many coping skills they can list within a set time limit to discuss as a class afterward. To practice these coping skills, the class can use some of the coping skills, such as breathing techniques, yoga, or dancing, to see how they make them feel. This can give students the awareness of the impact coping skills can have, and come to realize how they might help when they are feeling overwhelmed.

The class can suggest coping skills for the classroom that students can consider before stressful moments, such as taking a test or presenting in front of the class. The teacher can make a list or get a box to act as the class toolbox. The coping skills can be written on small sheets of paper, so when ready to use a coping skill, the teacher can pull one out for students to do. This can reinforce the idea of coping skills and give students a chance to calm their minds before an anxiety-provoking situation at school.

Week 8
Final Review and Toolbox Badge

Summary:

In this lesson, students will review coping skills and the superhero's toolbox they filled with coping skills to practice when big feelings are present. The class will sum up all they have learned within the last seven weeks. The teacher will have students teach the class the four different lessons (Anger Iceberg, Three Zones, ANTs, and Toolbox) learned throughout the curriculum, celebrating and awarding the class with their final badge, the Toolbox badge. The class will color and cut the badge to add to their Amy Hippo.

Objectives:
- Students will recognize and describe the purpose of the toolbox and coping skills lesson from the prior week
- Analyze the purpose and importance of learning the four different concepts
- Identify and describe each lesson learned throughout the curriculum

Time for lesson: 30-45 minutes

Resources and Supplies:
- Badges coloring page from Week Three
- Amy Hippo worksheet from Week One
- Color supplies
- Scissors
- Glue

Lesson Plan:

In this week's lesson, the teacher will start by reviewing coping skills and the Toolbox. Questions to consider:
- What is the purpose of having a toolbox filled with coping skills?
- What's a situation when we might need to access our toolboxes for a coping skill?

- What are some coping skills you can do at home or in a public setting, such as school or at a restaurant?
- What's a sign one's body shows when experiencing big emotions?
- What were some of the coping skills Becka and Amy Hippo learned?
- If someone saw a friend or family member starting to panic or feeling overwhelmed, what's something they could do or suggest to help them cope through it?
- Will everyone's toolbox look the same? Why or why not?

Once students demonstrate a grasp of coping skills and the Toolbox lesson, the class can discuss all that they have learned so far and what it means. Students have learned about big emotions, what they mean, and how to recognize and cope with them effectively through four new concepts (Anger Iceberg, Three Zones, ANTs, and The Toolbox). Each lesson has shown students a new way to understand and approach their emotions in a caring and mindful way. By the end of the curriculum, students are leaving with a new perspective and a plethora of skills to use and share.

With all of these new concepts, it's important to be able to share and teach them with others. The teacher will ask individual students, whether choosing student volunteers or picking names, to stand at the front of the classroom and teach one of the four concepts learned. Before starting, the class can practice the breathing technique Becka learned to calm their minds before presenting in front of the class. With each volunteer, the class can congratulate the "teacher" for the lesson.
The goal of each presentation is to have students actively participating and re-enforcing what they have learned to the class – approaching a nervous and anxious task, like Becka at the beginning of the story, but gaining the skills and confidence to share the concepts with others.

At the end of the student lessons, the teacher will award each student their Toolbox badge, their final badge of the curriculum. Students will end the lesson by coloring and cutting out their badge to add to their Amy Hippo collection. Once finished, the Amy Hippos will be collected or put away for their graduation day next week.

Conclusion:

At the end of this lesson, students will display mastery and confidence in the four concepts they have learned over the past weeks. Students will have recognized the significance of the lessons going into the last week of the curriculum. Earning their final badge, students will feel accomplished with their collection of badges and all of the skills they have acquired throughout the process.

Review:

- Review the Toolbox and coping skills lesson
- Reinforce the content students have learned and the skills they've mastered over the last weeks with student presentations on the four concepts
- Celebrate students with the final badge, The Toolbox badge
- Color and cut the last badge to glue onto their Amy Hippo

Modifications and Options:

With this lesson, the review and presentation process can be modified for each classroom. The review can be completed in any fashion that fits the class, such as having a gameshow style question and answer game, matching the different concepts and meaning to each other, or using more examples from media to pinpoint the character's emotions with each concept.

For the student presentations, students can work in four groups, each preparing a presentation or lesson for the rest of the class. This can be an informative presentation or a creative one with students using examples and commentary that is fitting to their humor. The presentations can also be broken down into different sections, considering how many students there are in a class and accounting for total participation. One student can explain the concept, the other describes how to address the feelings, and the last demonstrates an example of the concept (such as creating an Anger Iceberg for a character).

Before the presentations start, the teacher can suggest coping skills for students to practice before they go to present, such as breathing techniques, dancing, or small exercises. This will allow students to practice and apply coping skills, as well as ease them into the process of sharing with the class.

This week is focused on the review and having fun celebrating and showcasing all they have learned. The teacher can approach this week with their discretion, creating a fun atmosphere for the students to enjoy the curriculum thus far.

Week 9
Graduation Day

Summary:

In week nine, students will celebrate their achievements over the last nine weeks with a graduation party. The class will take home their Amy Hippos to keep and refer to, as well as to teach others the concepts they have learned. The teacher will then take a class picture with the students holding up their customized Amy Hippo. Displaying this group photo in the classroom for the remainder of the school year can serve as a visual reminder and reference point that the students now have the needed skills to overcome hard days as challenges arise within the classroom.

Objectives:
- Recognize and celebrate all the skills they have learned and badges they have earned
- Feel motivated to continue applying the skills and concepts they have learned in their lives
- Utilize skills in handling their emotions and moving through overwhelming situations
- Gain a partnership with their Amy Hippo, developing confidence in being in control rather than letting Amy Hippo take over

Time for lesson: 30 minutes

Resources and Supplies:
- Completed Amy Hippo worksheet from Week One
- Celebration supplies (snacks, drinks, balloons, etc.)

Lesson Plan:

This week's lesson is a big day for students. After eight weeks of gaining resourceful skills and mastering new concepts regarding big emotions and how to manage them, students will graduate as emotion superheroes, being able to face their emotions carefully and handle overwhelming situations with ease. Students will also be embarking on their journey with Amy Hippo, developing more control and a balanced relationship with their own little superhero. The lesson will be filled with positive affirmations and congratulations for the students, complimenting their progress and encouraging them on their journey.

At the end of the curriculum, students are in charge of their Amy Hippo, not having their emotions control their actions. They are now powerful enough to soothe their emotional responses and recognize their ability to handle the situations in front of them.

The teacher can celebrate students in many ways, such as bringing a snack, providing a class lunch, or having a dessert to surprise students with. Other options include playing music, putting on a movie, or having extra time at recess. The teacher can even decorate the classroom or have a real graduation with diplomas and paper graduation caps. This day can be celebrated to the teacher's liking and based on one's resources. In the end, the goal is to celebrate the students' accomplishments and participation in the curriculum. Before the end of the celebration, the teacher will take a class picture of the students holding their Amy Hippos. Students will take their Amy Hippo home to share all they have learned with friends and family, as well as serve as a reminder of all the skills and confidence they have gained over the curriculum.

Conclusion:

At the end of the lesson, students will go home feeling empowered to recognize and manage their emotions, as well as help others by sharing the skills they have learned. As students move on with the school year, they will find guidance and help through their new skills, increased emotional vocabulary, and confidence in their classroom as safe space for students to feel vulnerable and accepted when it comes to emotional skills management.

Review:

- Celebrate the class's achievements and their completion of the curriculum
- Take a class picture with everyone holding their Amy Hippo (to display in the classroom)
- Take Amy Hippo home

Modifications and Options:

With the graduation party, the teacher can decide how to celebrate their students that is fitting for their classroom and the available resources. There could be a pizza party or cake for students to enjoy. Though, purchasing things for the party is not the only option. Teachers can have activities and games for the students to do and play or let the students have a dance party. The goal of the party is to reward students for the accomplishments made in the last eight weeks. There can be a small graduation ceremony where parents are invited to join or students can teach another class the concepts they've mastered. This day can be decided by the teacher in any way they choose with plenty of creative options to celebrate their students.

Mental Health Counselors

Amy Hippo's Guide for Children's Mental Health Counseling Sessions

For clients that visit my office actively seeking support with emotional skills management and parent training, I start with a general outline for our expected 12-16 weeks together and customize each week's discussion and intervention based on the client's individual needs. Please note this general outline is intended to support clients that are not currently in crisis or experiencing suicidal ideation. This guide is best recommended for those deemed appropriate for introductory CBT interventions. The Amy Hippo course content is targeted towards elementary aged children and this guide presented is written for that audience. However, through my work, clients as old as 18 have requested to complete the Amy Hippo curriculum as well. For them, I share the curriculum graduation plan and their individual counseling treatment plans, allowing them to partner with me as we craft an Amy Hippo weekly plan that meets the needs of older adolescents. These plans will still allow them to gain the knowledge within the CBT concepts, display their own creativity, and take pride in their accomplishment through their own graduation style event in my office. I encourage you to adapt the curriculum guide to serve the individual needs within your office and to allow older children to experience the fun within this experience, should they express an interest as well.

Individual Client
Sample Amy Hippo Schedule

Date	Lesson Targets *(In-office session agenda)*	Weekly Missions *(homework)*
Week 1 (Intake assessment evaluation session)	**Welcome Day** – Meet Amy Hippo (& Clinician) Questions, more questions, introductions, paperwork and planning	-Purchase supplies -Color your hippo to share next week
Week 2	**Discuss:** The what, how & why of feelings **Lesson:** Anger Iceberg	-Client: Teach Anger Iceberg to someone at home -Bring real life examples of a completed iceberg next week (in your counseling journal)
Week 3 <u>**BADGE #1**</u>	**Review:** Counseling journal entries **Read:** Amy Hippo Part 1 (Flight) **Lesson:** My Three Zones **Discussion:** Body signs and language of anxiety – how does anxiety get bigger? Smaller?	-Client: Teach Three Zones at home to family -Record real life examples from the week of your experiences in each zone (logged in counseling journal)

Week 4	**Review:** Journal entries **Practice:** Iceberg & Three Zones case scenarios **Create:** Draw your own stuffed hippo	-Make a list of different things that woke up Amy Hippo for you this week (target: 5+ journal entries)
Week 5 **<u>BADGE #2</u>**	**Review:** Journal entries **Read:** Amy Hippo Part 2 (Freeze) **Create:** Cut out your own hippo	-Make a list of 3 or more things that triggered flight or freeze for you this week -Make a list of examples from other people, TV characters, or book characters
Week 6	**Review:** Journal entries **Read:** Amy Hippo Part 3 (Fight) **Practice:** Make an Anger Iceberg for Becka James **Lesson:** CBT Triangle intro **Create:** Final cuts/edits to your own hippo	**MOVIE NIGHT!** Watch the movie *Inside Out*, and complete the following missions: 1.Pick a scene to make an Iceberg 2.Pick a scene to draw Riley's Three Zones and place a dot to represent how far Riley was pushed outside her comfort zone 3.Did Riley's Amy Hippo wake up and try to save her by flight, fight, or freeze? Journal about any you find

Week 7 Bring your toolbox	**Review:** Movie Night journal entries **Read:** Amy Hippo Part 4 (Coping) **Discuss:** How will you fill your toolbox?	-Teach coping skills to someone at home -Journal a list of the coping skills you taught others and the ones you used for yourself this week
Week 8 **BADGE #3**	**Review:** Coping Skills and Journal **Lesson:** ANTs & CBT Triangle **Create:** Fill your toolbox **Create:** Stuff your own hippo	-Practice using your toolbox -Journal a list of the tools used and when you knew they were needed
Week 9 **BADGE #4**	**Discuss:** What's in my toolbox? Growth recap **Reverse!** Client becomes the counselor & teaches the counselor the main concepts learned during the counseling process **Create:** Stuff and finalize your own hippo	Pick your own mission:

Week 10	**Option 1:** Family session for parent training and to review growth and concerns. OR **Option 2:** Flex Day to strengthen concepts and complete any missed home tasks or outstanding items	**Family Mission!** Parents/Guardians make a list in client's journal of the things they're proud of this week (Did the client use their toolbox when needed? Did they communicate needs/feelings effectively? Did they interrupt and soothe their Amy Hippo when anxiety started to appear? List them all to share next week!)
Week 11 **<u>BADGE #5</u>**	**Review:** Journal entries **Practice:** CBT case scenarios	Reflect and seek moments to feel proud of yourself for using your new Amy Hippo skills
Week 12	**GRADUATION DAY!!** Let's celebrate your big achievement with cake, hippos, and family Great work! You're now in charge of your Amy Hippo! She doesn't get to control you anymore	Bring your own hippo home as a reminder that you're now powerful enough to calm Amy Hippo down anytime she tries to save you when you don't truly need her help

<u>Client Supply List:</u>

- Journal - needed at every session
- Toolbox (*small box of any type*)

Week 1
Welcome Day

Summary:

    In this session, the counselor will meet with the client and their parents or guardians to introduce themselves and explain the Amy Hippo course they will be completing over the next few months. The counselor will explain how the sessions work and what the client has to look forward to during this process. Clients will meet Amy Hippo and color their own Amy Hippo to share in the next session. The counselor will complete the needed evaluations and assessments, develop a client treatment plan, and list the supplies needed for the course.

Objectives:
- Familiarize counseling plan and course with clients and their parents/guardians
- Engage the client with the activities and events in the upcoming sessions
- Ease client and parents into the counseling plan
- Complete an intake evaluation and assessment form and treatment plan before the next session
- Encourage the client to color their own Amy Hippo to share in the next session

Supplies:
- Amy Hippo Counseling Schedule
- Amy Hippo coloring sheet – (page 98 & online PDF download)

Session Plan:

    In the first counseling session, the counselor will meet with the client and their parents or guardians and introduce the Amy Hippo curriculum the client will be working on over the next couple of months. This curriculum will act as supplemental activities and lessons to the client's individual talk therapy session. Clients will also meet Amy Hippo, a superhero hippo whose mission is to help her best friend through overwhelming emotions and moments. Everyone has an Amy Hippo (the brain's **amy**gdala and **hippo**campus) looking out for them, and in this course, the client will be making their own Amy Hippo to keep and look to for guidance. However, Amy Hippo needs some training to help her best friend with big emotions. Over the course, clients will be learning the skills to better recognize and handle these big emotions, training their Amy Hippo along the way.

The counselor can highlight the exciting parts of individual counseling and the Amy Hippo curriculum. Not only will they get to make their own Amy Hippo to take home, but they will also have a big graduation party at the end of the course to celebrate their achievements throughout the sessions. Clients can leave knowing how to make their big emotions and these hard days a little easier to handle and more manageable through all the skills they have gained and concepts they have learned over the course. Not only can they use these skills in their lives, but they can also teach others how to face their big emotions. This will help excite clients with all they have to look forward to and work toward, but also show parents or guardians that the counseling experience does not have to be a life-long commitment, and instead can be a learning process for their child to continue using after the sessions are completed.

Counselors will complete an intake evaluation and assessment with the client. It is recommended for counselors to continue implementing the intake evaluation and assessment protocol put in place for their individual practice. Counselors can use this guide as an add-on or additional supplemental material to their established CBT therapy sessions.

Counselors will move on to creating a treatment plan for the client. Using this guide, counselors can utilize components of the Amy Hippo course within the client's treatment plan, if desired, modifying the Amy Hippo material to fit the individual client's needs. This guide is adjustable and adaptable for counselors to work into a client's session and treatment plan.

The counselor will ask the client's parents or guardians to bring the two supplies needed for the course to the next session. Clients will need a journal of their choosing to complete assignments in – a spiral notebook or a binder with notebook paper will do - anything for the client to write in. The client will also need a small box – anything from a cardboard box to one from a craft or hardware store will suffice. This box will be utilized during the "Toolbox" lesson where students will fill their box with different coping skills to pull from when feeling overwhelmed or facing big emotions. The client can make their box or decorate it any way they like.

The session will end with the counselor giving the client an Amy Hippo coloring sheet to color and decorate to share in the next counseling session.

Review:
- Meet with the client and their parents or guardians to introduce the counseling sessions, the Amy Hippo course, and Amy Hippo herself
- Discuss the activities and events to look forward to over the next 12-16 weeks
- Complete an intake evaluation and assessment and a treatment plan for the client
- List supplies needed for the course
- Provide Amy Hippo coloring page for the client to color and share in their next session

Note to Counselor:
Throughout the Amy Hippo counseling course, the client will be making a physical Amy Hippo to take home on graduation day. The Amy Hippo crafting project initially started as a stuffed animal Amy Hippo. The client would help trace and cut out the fabric pieces for the counselor to sew together at the end of the lesson. However, not all counselors will have the skills or resources to do this project for each client. There are many ways to make a physical Amy Hippo for the client to work on. An Amy Hippo can be made by cutting out felt and

creating a small stuffed hippo, using modeling clay for clients to sculpt their Amy Hippo, building their hippo with Legos, or using recycled material to craft into a hippo. This is a place to get creative and play with ways the client can make an Amy Hippo in an interactive, hands-on fashion. Find the means that work best for you given the resources you can acquire, the different skills you may have, and what will work best for your client.

Week 2
Feelings and The Anger Iceberg

Summary:

In this session, the counselor will facilitate a discussion on emotions. Clients will be introduced to Anger Icebergs, applying the concept to their counseling session discussion. The client will share their colored Amy Hippo from the previous session. For the client's weekly mission, the counselor will task the client to practice Anger Icebergs using real life examples from the week, creating entries in their journal.

Objectives:
- Discuss the different emotions in the client's presenting concerns, analyzing what they mean, how they affect one's life, and why they occur
- Introduce clients to The Anger Iceberg concept, familiarizing the client with secondary anger responses and the primary emotions hidden beneath the surface
- Encourage clients to discuss the topics learned after the counseling session
- Complete a journal entry at home, using real-life examples to practice the Anger Iceberg concept and share in the next session

Supplies:
- Anger Iceberg worksheet (pg 101 & online as PDF)

Session Plan:

In this session, the counselor can introduce the topic of emotions, familiarizing the client with what emotions are and facilitating a deeper dive into the meaning behind them. The counselor can use the concept of big emotions in the client's talk therapy session, discussing the where, what, and why of the emotions they experienced that week.

People have a broad and rich emotional experience in their daily living, but how often do they pause to consider what these feelings mean or why they might feel a certain emotion? Recognizing these feelings can allow one to become more mindful of what they are experiencing in any given situation, approaching these feelings with more clarity and means to ease or manage them. Learning the ins and outs of emotions can make them feel less overwhelming and intimidating, helping people face their feelings calmly and with more control.

Based on the client's session, the counselor can introduce Anger Icebergs to the discussion, focusing on outward displays of emotions versus one's internal and hidden experiences of emotions. The counselor can reference a troubling moment from the client's week where they reacted with displays of anger, prompting the client to dig deeper and spot what they were feeling beneath the anger. On the tip of the iceberg, just floating over the water, the client will place the word "anger," a secondary emotion. The tip of the iceberg represents the big emotion we feel secure in showing to the outside world. In the world of mental health care, anger is often referred to as a "secondary emotion" because in our Western society, anger is generally seen as commonplace and not often associated with weakness or vulnerability, therefore, it can feel fairly safe for us to display outward anger. Anger is often fueled by primary emotions that frequently provoke sensations of vulnerability when expressed openly. Therefore, primary feelings of shame or fear may instead be expressed with the secondary response of anger as a defense against this vulnerability.

For example, you did something embarrassing at school and everyone laughed. Your first reaction visible to others might be anger, but inside you feel embarrassed, ashamed, worthless, or sad. You might not understand why you feel this way or don't want to show this to your friends and peers since allowing increased vulnerability in a public setting can feel intimidating and scary in itself. So, instead you immediately react with anger, allowing that secondary emotional response.

Allow your client to consider all the emotions they masked on the inside and list them on the part of the iceberg underneath the surface.

For the weekly mission, the counselor will ask the client to complete an Anger Iceberg for a situation they experienced that week where their big emotion took over.

Review:

- Discuss the what, how, and why of feelings based on situations discussed in the counseling session
- Introduce the Anger Iceberg concept and incorporate it into the session if useful, practicing with a situation the client faced that week
- Task client to teach others the Anger Icebergs concept and to create one using a real-life example from the week

Note to Counselor:

It is encouraged for counselors to discuss and teach these lessons in the style and fashion they see fit for the client. It's important for the counselor to continue with their sessions and format, using the Amy Hippo curriculum as an add-on or integrated feature to the sessions. The counselor can adapt the content to fit their methods and teaching style using their worksheets, examples, or explanations in their sessions. This curriculum can easily be adjusted to accommodate the counselor and the client.

There is additional information on the website at www.amyhippo.com and an Anger Iceberg worksheet available on page 101 or as a PDF download online.

Week 3
Anger Iceberg Badge and Three Zones

Summary:

In this session, the counselor will review and discuss the client's Anger Iceberg journal entry. They will award the client their first badge, the Anger Iceberg badge, to color and cut. The counselor and client will read the first story in A*my Hippo: The Superhero Who Tried Too Hard*, "Part One: Flight". After completing the discussion questions, the counselor will introduce the Three Zones concept to the client, using examples from the session to explain the meaning of each zone. The counselor will discuss body signs and the language of anxiety, analyzing the ways one's body reacts to anxiety and other big emotions. The client will be assigned their weekly lesson, teaching the Three Zones to their friends or family and using real life examples from the week to place or categorize into the Three Zones.

Objectives:

- Demonstrate an understanding of the Anger Iceberg through the weekly mission assignment, earning their Anger Iceberg badge
- Read and discuss "Part One: Flight", analyzing Becka's moment in the classroom and answering discussion questions about moments of feeling scared or embarrassed
- Engage with the new concept, the Three Zones, using examples from the client's session to further an understanding of the concept
- Discuss body signs and the language of anxiety, sharing examples of physiological signals of anxiety and panic
- Encourage clients to share the Three Zones with family or friends and use the Three Zones to label and categorize real-life examples from the week

Supplies:

- *Amy Hippo: The Superhero Who Tried Too Hard*, "Part One: Flight"
- Three Zones worksheet (page 102 & online as PDF)
- Badge worksheet (page 100 & online as PDF)
- Coloring supplies
- Scissors
- Hole punch
- String (twine, yarn, etc.)

Session Plan:

In this lesson, the client will share their journal entry on Anger Icebergs, discussing the moment they chose and how they were able to pinpoint the emotions felt under the surface. The counselor can prompt the client to think of ways they could have calmed down their anger or how they might have reacted if their focus was on communicating the emotions happening beneath the surface. After showing an understanding of the Anger Iceberg, the counselor will award the client their first badge of the curriculum, the Anger Iceberg badge.

This is a celebratory moment for the client, earning their first skills badge to add to their Amy Hippo at the end of the course. The client should feel excited and proud of this accomplishment and eager to achieve the other badges awaiting them in the upcoming sessions.

The counselor and client can read "Part One: Flight", the first story of the reading material in the curriculum. The client will meet Becka James and her superhero, Amy Hippo. Though for Becka, Amy Hippo only seems to make her life harder, helping her out at all the wrong times. The counselor and client will discuss the situation Becka faces in class, panicking and running out of the classroom after being called to answer a math problem on the board. At this moment, Becka was overcome with anxious and embarrassed feelings, standing before the entire class, causing her Amy Hippo to swoop in and help her by pulling her from the situation.

The counselor can discuss the story with the client, breaking down what happened to Becka and why Amy Hippo decided to "help" her at that moment. The counselor can move on to the discussion questions after the story to talk about moments in the client's life where they might have felt anxious or embarrassed themselves, relating those moments to how Becka might have felt in the story.

During the session, the counselor can introduce the Three Zones concept to the client's session. The Three Zones symbolize the three stages of emotional experiences we find ourselves in across varying situations. The first zone, right in the middle of the target, is the **Comfort and Safety Zone** – a zone where we feel comfortable and most at ease, like at home with our feet up or reading in the park. We can relax and recharge in this zone because nothing is challenging or pushing us and we are safe here. This zone is important to help us relax and recharge daily and gives us time to release tensions and let our guard down. Though this stage sounds nice and easy, we are not growing in this zone so it's important to routinely move beyond the Comfort and Safety Zone. It's also vital that we return to this zone to unwind and embrace feeling secure in our space. In the next zone, we are moved to a less comfortable space filled with possibilities for personal growth and discovery. The **Growth and Learning Zone** is a zone where one is ready to engage and be focused on new situations and ideas.

Whether in school or social situations, the Growth and Learning Zone encourages being present and willing to act and interact. Though being a stage of growing as a person and experiencing new situations, one can feel anxious in the moment, especially being faced with unfamiliar things. It's important to normalize these feelings of anxiety. It's natural to feel a bit of anxiety going into a new situation, but these uncertain feelings will eventually subside the more you do it and allow yourself to grow through difficult moments with more ease in the future. Yet, in the final zone, the final ring of the target, the feelings of anxiety and worry, once felt in the Growth and Learning Zone, reach an emergency level, hindering one's progress. This zone, the **Fear and Anger Zone**, affects the logical side of your brain, turning off all rationale and the thinking part of your brain and instead using the emotional side to respond. In other words, your survival instinct is kicked into gear.

It's easy to cross into the Fear and Anger Zone as you respond only from your emotional (survival mode) side – similar to the Anger Iceberg, only responding with anger without considering everything else going on. This is where Amy Hippo comes to swoop in – the emergency emotional response side of your brain is the Amy Hippo control center. From here, Amy Hippo (your brain's **amy**gdala and **hippo**campus) only allows you to react with fight, flight or freeze. In these moments, if you are not in immediate danger, it is important to find ways to move back to the middle zone to continue one's growth and positive handling of new situations. This will become achievable with the aid of personal coping skills taught in the upcoming weeks of this course.

An optional Three Zones worksheet is available online at www.amyhippo.com or on page 102. To complete the worksheet, instruct your client to color each zone a different color and write one example of an experience that fits each zone. For example, color the Comfort and Safety Zone green and write "napping" or "movie night" in the center most zone. Next, color the Learning and Growth Zone yellow and write "school" or "soccer practice" as the experience. Then, color the Fear and Panic Zone red and write a possible example of "riding a new rollercoaster" or "getting in trouble". Last, instruct your client to draw their own facial expressions in the boxes below from the examples they provided for each zone. This will allow them to see how their body and facial expressions change as they move into different zones.

The counselor can teach the client this concept by having them pinpoint what zone they are in now and what zones they experienced during the personal situations they discussed in the session. Discussing these zones, the counselor can ask the client what caused them to enter a certain zone, what they were feeling at the moment, and how they might be able to move out of that zone if facing a similar situation. The counselor can talk about body signs and the language of anxiety with the client. Looking back at the story, Becka experienced many different feelings in her body. These feelings were signals her body was sending to her brain, alerting Amy Hippo to take action. Feelings of anxiety and panic can cause several types of physiological responses including; sweating, fidgeting, tightened muscles, and shallow breathing, which can ultimately engage the body's natural survival responses of flight, fight, or freeze. Considering the session, the counselor can ask the client to analyze a moment where they faced anxiety and what they felt in the moment. At that moment, was there anything that made the anxiety bigger or smaller? What could have caused the anxiety to escalate, or even subside?

When situations build on each other, anxiety can grow in the moment. Just like with Becka, her anxiety started after being called by Mr. Twiddlebug, waking her from her daydreaming, to answer the problem on the board. However, her anxiety grew while standing in front of her classmates. The counselor can ask the client what could have happened, or what Becka could have done, to help minimize her anxiety.

In the session, the counselor will have the client color and cut their first badge. After the badge is finished, the counselor will cut a piece of string and hole punch the badge to thread onto the string. At the end of the Amy Hippo curriculum, the client will have earned all five badges, coloring, and cutting them to be placed all on one piece of string. This string of badges will be tied around the Amy Hippo the client makes throughout the sessions, acting as Amy Hippo's collar.

The weekly mission asks for the client to teach the Three Zones to family or friends, showcasing their knowledge of the concept and recognizing the different zones people are in. In their journal, the client will take moments from the week and recognize which zone they were in.

Review:
- Review and discuss the client's journal entry, awarding the client the Anger Iceberg badge for their understanding of the concept
- Read "Part One: Flight", discussing the events of the story and feelings of embarrassment and worry
- Introduce the Three Zones concept, incorporating the different zones into the counseling session

- Discuss body signs and the feeling of anxiety
- Task the client with their weekly mission, teaching the Three Zones to others and listing moments from the week to pinpoint what zone they were present in
- Color and cut badge to add to a piece of string

Note to Counselor:

With this course, the client will not always move through the schedule at the same pace. A client may come to this week's session needing more support with Anger Icebergs or a session dedicated to a new issue they are facing. This might push them back a week, however, the curriculum adapts to every client's needs and pace. This course can take the twelve weeks or it could take more depending on the client. This should not discourage the client from continuing forward – rather, they are right on track with where they need to be. Each lesson might take more or less time for a client, as long as they are taking in the concept and taking the right time for them to understand it and apply it to their life. The client will still earn all five badges and have their graduation party at the end.

As seen at the end of "Part One", there are Amy Hippo discussion questions for readers to answer and consider. The counselor can work on the discussion questions with the client or have the client write, draw, or tell a story for their responses. It's a moment for the client to discuss questions about the story and emotions in any way that works best for them, whether a moment of creativity or dialogue.

The coloring of the badge can be done at any point in the session. It can be held for the end of the session or be completed during discussion. Coloring and hands-on projects can help clients when sharing, focusing their eyes on the project in front of them instead of maintaining eye contact – something everyone can find a bit intimidating and anxiety-inducing. Having a hands-on project can help some clients focus better on the lessons being taught, keeping their bodies busy and opening their minds to learn.

Week 4
Practice and Draw Amy Hippo

Summary:

In this session, the counselor will review and discuss the client's journal entry on the Three Zones. The counselor and client can practice Anger Icebergs and Three Zones with examples from the client's session. The client will work on crafting their Amy Hippo to take home at the end of the curriculum. The counselor will assign the client's weekly mission, making a list of different things or moments that woke up their Amy Hippo during the week.

Objectives:
- Showcase an understanding of the Anger Iceberg and Three Zones from the journal entry and through practiced examples
- Make progress on the client's Amy Hippo craft project
- Encourage clients to recognize moments that stirred their Amy Hippo into action

Supplies:
- Amy Hippo crafting material

Session Plan:

In this session, the counselor will review the client's Three Zones journal entry, discussing the zones they experienced. The counselor can prompt the client to describe how each zone they experienced felt and what they did or could have done to move from one zone to another.

Depending on the session, the counselor can use the Anger Iceberg and Three Zones concepts to help break down situations and moments discussed throughout the client's therapy session. This allows the client to further their awareness and visual understanding of their emotions and processing of emotions, as well as broaden their comprehension of the two concepts.

This week the client will begin working on crafting their Amy Hippo to take home at the end of the curriculum. For the stuffed or felt hippo, the client will start drawing out the hippo from a template or an example. With other crafts, the client can start forming their Hippo out of the material the counselor chooses – such as clay, recycled material, or craft paper. The hands-on crafting process can be done at the end or during the session, allowing clients to interact with a project while participating in their talk therapy and curriculum practice.

The client's weekly mission is to list the things that woke up their Amy Hippo during the week. Amy Hippo jumps into action when someone faces big emotions where one's body starts sending emergency signals to the brain that danger is present. Amy Hippo might swoop in when her human is feeling escalating anxiety, panic, or fear that turns off the logical side and engages the survival mode responses. The client's Amy Hippo might swoop in at an attempt to protect them from the perceived dangerous situation by triggering a fight, flight, or freeze response. The client's goal is to have at least five moments on the list, though they can list as many as they desire.

Review:

- Review and discuss the client's journal entry on the Three Zones
- Practice Three Zones and Anger Iceberg concepts within the counseling session
- Start creating the client's personalized Amy Hippo project
- Task the client with their weekly mission, creating a list of things that caused the client's Amy Hippo to stir into action throughout the week

Note to Counselor:

The client can use the concepts and vocabulary learned in the course during the talk therapy portion of the session. To practice the concepts and encourage clients to use them as a visual guide, the counselor can ask clients to create an Anger Iceberg for certain situations they faced and discussed in their session. They might make an Anger Iceberg for how they reacted and one for the other person involved in the situation, breaking down what was truly being felt on both sides. They can consider a moment they felt panicked by something new, recognizing how they moved into the Anger and Fear Zone and how they could move back into the Growth and Learning Zone. The concepts can be incorporated into the client's understanding of their emotions and reactions in the situations they bring to the session, and further their grasp on emotions and how to effectively manage and communicate them.

Week 5
Three Zones Badge and Part Two

Summary:

In this session, the counselor will review and discuss the client's journal entry focusing on triggers that alerted their Amy Hippo. The counselor and the client will read "Part Two: Freeze" and discuss the ways they could help Becka with her overwhelming situation. The client's weekly mission is to make a list of things that triggered a flight or freeze reaction for them during the week, as well as make the same list for a person in their life or a fictional character. The client will be awarded the Three Zones badge to color, cut, and add to their badge collection.

Objectives:
- Discuss the things that happened that week that alerted their Amy Hippo, analyzing the body signals they felt and how their Amy Hippo helped
- Identify what caused Becka to freeze during her soccer game and consider how one could help Becka after the game
- List situations that resulted in flight or freeze responses during the week, exploring if these reactions helped with their emotions or the situation

Supplies:
- *Amy Hippo: The Superhero Who Tried Too Hard,* "Part Two: Freeze"
- Amy Hippo craft project
- Badge worksheet from Week Three
- Coloring supplies
- Scissors
- Hole punch
- Badge string

Session Plan:

In this session, the counselor will review the list of things that triggered the client's Amy Hippo to wake up and be on alert. In these situations, the client can explain what body signals they might have felt or examine the pattern of emotions they were feeling with the situations they faced. How did they handle these situations, and did their Amy Hippo help them in any way?

The counselor can work on reading "Part Two: Freeze" with the client. In this story, Becka is assigned to be the goalie for her soccer team's first game. However, as her nerves start to sneak up on her and her mind starts to wander, she fails to block the other team from making a goal. Becka begins experiencing escalating physiological responses (chest and shoulders tightened, shaking hands, racing heart) until Amy Hippo swoops in to save her, leaving Becka frozen as the other team scores another goal. At this moment, Amy Hippo was just trying to help Becka, but by the end of the story, Becka only feels worse and worried she let her team down. Becka's body was sending signals to her brain, turning off the logical side and tapping into the emotional side, the Amy Hippo control center. Her emotions naturally caused her to freeze during a stressful moment when she needed to help her team win. The counselor can ask the client about moments they froze or ran away from a situation in their life – did it help with their emotions or save them from an overwhelming moment?

The counselor and the client can answer questions from the "Amy Asks" section after the story, discussing how the client would have helped Becka at that moment and what her teammates might have been thinking about Becka after the game. The client can put themselves in Becka's shoes or in the perspective of the teammates, helping her get through her overwhelming emotions and doubts.

The client's weekly mission is to list three or more things that triggered flight or freeze for the client during the week. When experiencing panic, one sends physiological signals to their brain that danger is present and the brain's amygdala and hippocampus reacts to protect them in these moments. Recognizing and pinpointing this experience can help clients become more aware of when their body reacts this way. The counselor can task the client to make a list of triggering moments for a family member, friend, or character from a movie, TV show, or book. The client can recognize the universality of these emotional reactions as well as what causes these reactions to occur.

After their practice last week, the client will be awarded the Three Zones badge. They will be able to color and cut out the badge to add to their string of badges for Amy Hippo's collar.

Review:
- Review and discuss the client's journal entry on events that resulted in their Amy Hippo waking up
- Read "Part Two: Freeze" and discuss what happened to Becka in the story
- Task the client with their weekly mission, creating a list of moments that triggered a personal flight or freeze reaction that week and one for a family member, friend, or fictional character
- Award Three Zones badge to color, cut, and add to their collection of badges

Note to Counselor:
With the curriculum reading material, the counselor can read through the book with the client or have it be an additional weekly mission to read one of the parts to discuss in the session. However, if read during the session, the counselor can relate the story and experiences of the main character to the client and the topics they bring to the session. The client might not have found themselves in the same situation before, but the feelings and emotions might be familiar to the client in some fashion. The book sections can be an activity that happens naturally within the session rather than being a requirement, allowing the client a pause from the talk therapy to continue exploring themes of big emotions and how to manage them.

For the discussion questions, the client can answer based on their understanding of the story or approach the questions given situations and emotions they have experienced. The story and discussion questions can coincide with the client's needs and what they bring to the sessions to further expand and focus on the client's treatment plan.

Week 6
CBT Triangle and Movie Night

Summary:

In this session, the counselor will review the client's weekly journal entry, discussing the list of triggering events of flight or freeze the client made for themselves and a family member, friend, or fictional character. The counselor and the client can move to the next section of the curriculum reading material, "Part Three: Fight", discussing Becka's big emotional reaction at her family's dinner. Based on the events of the reading, the client will be tasked to make an Anger Iceberg for Becka, deciding the emotions she experienced underneath her outward display of anger. The counselor will introduce the CBT Triangle concept during the client's talk therapy session and discuss the relationship between thoughts, feelings, and behaviors. The client will continue to work on their Amy Hippo creation, making the final edits to their hippo before finishing it in Week Nine. For the client's weekly mission, they will be assigned to watch the Pixar movie, *Inside Out*. In their journal, the client will practice making an Anger Iceberg, drawing and pointing out the Three Zones target, and finding active Amy Hippo moments in scenes and characters throughout the film.

Objectives:
- Discuss triggering events, recognizing what the client felt in moments of flight or freeze
- Analyze why someone or a character might have experienced the triggering events of flight or freeze the client listed
- Participate in reading and discussing the events of the story and the changes the client would make to the situation the character faced
- Develop an Anger Iceberg for the main character based on an understanding of the events of the story
- Discuss the CBT Triangle concept, illustrating the cyclical process of thoughts, feelings, and behaviors

- Progress with the client's Amy Hippo craft project, moving closer to finishing the project
- Complete weekly mission, analyzing the assigned movie and completing journal entries based on the scenes and characters in the film

Supplies:

- *Amy Hippo: The Superhero Who Tried Too Hard,* "Part Three: Fight"
- Anger Iceberg worksheet (page 101 & online PDF)
- Amy Hippo project from Week Four
- Project supplies

Session Plan:

This week, the counselor will review the entries the client made over the week. Looking at the client's list of flight or freeze responses and what triggered these reactions, the counselor can discuss what the client physically and mentally experienced in those moments. What did each response look like and what patterns can they spot in their reactions and triggers? Considering their second list for someone they know or a character, the counselor can ask the client to give their perspective of what happened to the person during the triggering moment and how they could help the person soothe the impulse of flight or freeze.

The counselor and client can continue with the curriculum material, reading "Part Three: Fight". Overwhelmed by the events of the day so far and the rampant negative thoughts in her head, Becka zones out at her family dinner, only to be scolded by her parents for not paying attention and ignoring everyone at the table. Amy Hippo notices Becka is overwhelmed by her emotions and decides to spring into action. However, her help causes Becka to react in anger, flinging her food across the table. At this moment, Becka has a multitude of feelings and Automatic Negative Thoughts (ANTs) brewing within her – upset from the day and doubtful of herself. Rather than addressing these emotions, she is stuck in her one big feeling, reacting only from the emotional side of her brain. She acts out in anger, but this is not the only feeling she is experiencing. Looking toward the discussion questions, the client is prompted to consider what was wrong with Becka and what they could do to help her at this moment.

The counselor will ask the client to make an Anger Iceberg for Becka and her reaction at dinner. She reacted with her big emotion, anger, but what was she feeling underneath the surface? How did the events of the day lead to this moment? The client can consider the Anger Icebergs they created in previous sessions or similar situations they faced where they were overcome by a big emotion of anger despite having more unaddressed feelings under the surface.

The CBT Triangle will be the next concept introduced into the lesson. The counselor can explain the CBT Triangle to the client and the cyclical pattern of one's thoughts, feelings, and behaviors. The counselor can illustrate the concept using situations the client has brought to the sessions, showcasing the nature of how one's thoughts can influence one's feelings which will then influence one's behavior only to repeat the process if no steps are taken to interrupt the cycle. By recognizing one's patterns using the CBT Triangle, one can take the action to correct the pattern through consistent positive action or with the help of a mental health professional. Together the counselor and client can create a CBT Triangle for a certain situation the client faced to illustrate the process of how the client's thoughts, feelings, and behavior affected one another.

In the session, the client will continue working on their Amy Hippo project, making the final cuts and edits based on the type of crafting project they are doing. This week, the client will be close to finishing their Amy Hippo and will complete the final touches in a couple weeks.

For the client's weekly mission, they are tasked to have a movie night, watching the film *Inside Out* (2015). After watching the film, the client has three tasks to complete based on the scenes and main character of the movie.

1. Pick a scene to make an Anger Iceberg – considering the characters in the scene, decide what emotion they are showing openly and what emotions they are feeling under the surface.

2. Pick a scene to draw Riley's Three Zones, placing a dot to represent how far Riley was pushed outside her comfort zone – considering how receptive Riley was to new situations and experiences, whether accepting of the situation or moving into a panicked feeling.

3. Recognize if Riley's Amy Hippo woke up and tried to save her with flight, fight, or freeze – discussing what they find in the movie and what happened to Riley at the moment.

Review:

- Review and discuss the client's journal entry on the list of things that triggered flight or freeze that week for themselves and someone else
- Read "Part Three: Fight", discussing what happened to Becka and how the client would have changed the story to help Becka
- Task the client to make an Anger Iceberg for Becka during her situation at dinner
- Introduce and practice the CBT Triangle
- Continue to work on the client's Amy Hippo project, making the final cuts and edits
- Assign this week's task of watching *Inside Out* and answering questions based on the scenes and main character

Note to Counselor:

For this lesson, the counselor can reinforce the concepts behind Cognitive Behavioral Therapy to the client to clarify the importance of the CBT Thought-Feeling-Behavior Triangle. The counselor can share their experience with the practice and the techniques and elements they implement in their sessions. This can further inform the client about the concept and open their eyes to the different factors of their counseling sessions.

The client should be making progress on their Amy Hippo project to finalize in the following weeks. However, if the client is still working on their hippo and needs more time on the project, the counselor can set a time in the next sessions for the client to continue working. Talk therapy and teaching new concepts can still be implemented during this crafting time. The client can work hands-on, taking away some of the pressure and anxiety of talking about themselves and answering questions.

The counselor might want to inform the client and their parents or guardians of the movie night in advance. This will allow the parents or guardians time to acquire the movie from the library or a friend if need be.

Week 7
Coping Skills and Toolbox

Summary:

In the session, the counselor will review the client's movie night, discussing the movie and the concepts they used to explore the emotions of the characters and scenes. The counselor and the client can continue to read "Part Four: Superhero's Toolbox", discussing coping skills and how they feel about their Amy Hippo. On the topic of coping skills, the client will learn more about the meaning and purpose of coping skills. For the client's weekly mission, they will be teaching what coping skills are at home, listing the ones they taught others, the ones they used themselves, and when they knew to use them.

Objectives:

- Demonstrate an understanding of the emotional responses occurring in the film
- Consider the different coping skills Becka learned and examine the importance of training one's Amy Hippo
- Develop a list of coping skills to utilize when faced with overwhelming feelings and situations
- Practice teaching and utilizing coping skills at home, explaining how they knew when to use them and how they benefited in certain situations

Supplies:

- *Amy Hippo: The Superhero Who Tried Too Hard,* "Part Four: Superhero's Toolbox"
- Toolbox (client supply)

Session Plan:

In this session, the counselor will review the client's entries analyzing the different characters and situations in the film using the concepts learned so far in the sessions. The counselor can discuss with the client what they thought about the film and the emotions Riley faced. Were there any moments or emotions from the movie the client experienced in their life? How would they help Riley with what she was feeling?

The counselor and client can continue reading the final part of the curriculum reading material, "Part Four: Superhero's Toolbox". Becka, down on her luck with her Amy Hippo, seeks answers as to why her Amy Hippo only makes her life harder. With the help of her friends, Becka realizes that Amy Hippo was trying to help her all along. In overwhelming situations, Becka's body sends signals to her brain, alerting her Amy Hippo to jump into action. These overwhelming situations and body signals cause Becka's logical side to turn off, activating her emotional side, the Amy Hippo control center, to respond to the situation. Amy Hippo tries to help Becka from being hurt in situations, yet in doing so, makes Becka react only with her emotional side instead of with her more rational side. Becka decides to enroll her and Amy Hippo into classes to help both of them learn skills on how to cope with overwhelming emotions and situations, as well as how to work better together. In the end, Becka can handle her emotions with more control, while Amy Hippo can continue to cheer her on.

The counselor can use the therapy session to discuss moments where the client's Amy Hippo jumped into action, and ways they could have soothed and coped with those emotions before Amy Hippo took over. Looking at the discussion, the client is asked what they feel about their Amy Hippo, whether they are proud, frustrated, or indifferent to her. Given the topics the client brings to the session, the client might have negative opinions of their Amy Hippo. However, with this session, the client can learn new skills to help take more control over their Amy Hippo to have a peaceful partnership with her.

In the discussion, the client is asked to expand on additional coping skills. The counselor can look for moments in the session where a coping skill might have been helpful at the moment before the client's emotions took over, taking a moment to make a list of coping skills that have worked in the past for the client or things that help calm them down or distract their minds for a moment. Considering those moments, how would using a coping skill help that situation or change the outcome?

The client will be asked to bring in the box from their supply list to use in the next session to fill with these coping skills.

This week's mission tasks the client to teach coping skills at home to family and friends, sharing the different coping skills discussed in the session. In their journal, the client will be asked to make a list of coping skills they taught or shared with others as well as the ones they used that week, listing the tools they used and explaining when they knew to use them.

Review:

- Review the client's Movie Night journal entries, looking at the different concepts used to analyze scenes and characters
- Read "Part Four: Superhero's Toolbox", discussing coping skills and the purpose of Amy Hippo
- Introduce coping skills within the counseling session discussion, listing new coping skills for future use by the client
- For the weekly mission, task the client to teach coping skills to someone at home, listing the ones they taught and the ones they utilized that week

Note to Counselor:

In the session, the counselor can practice coping skills with the client to show them how to utilize these tools, as well as explore and discuss the effect it had on them. An easy one to practice is the breathing technique shown in the book. This can be an introduction to coping skills for the client to practice and experience the immediate impacts of implementing coping strategies.

Week 8
ANTs, CBT Triangle, Badge, and Toolbox

Summary:
In this session, the counselor will review the client's journal entry, discussing the different skills they taught others and used for themselves that week. The counselor will review the CBT Triangle and introduce ANTs, Automatic Negative Thoughts, into the client's counseling discourse. They will work on listing coping skills to add to their toolbox to pull from when things get overwhelming. The client will be awarded their third badge, the Toolbox badge, to color, cut, and add to their badge collection. The client will continue to work on their Amy Hippo crafting project, stuffing or putting the final touches on their project. For the client's weekly mission, they will practice using the toolbox, making a list of the tools they used and when they knew to use them.

Objectives:
- Recognize the different coping skills the client used during the week and how they helped in the situation
- Introduce the ANTs concept, developing an understanding of the concept and recognizing the ANTs present in the client's life
- Review CBT Triangle, building awareness and comprehension of how one's thoughts, feelings, and behaviors affect each other in a cyclical process
- Comprise the coping skills they listed and used last week to add to their toolbox to actively pull from in future situations
- Progress on their Amy Hippo project, applying their creative skills and being productive in the final steps of the project
- Utilize their toolbox when facing overwhelming emotions, recognizing when they knew to use a coping tool

Supplies:
- Paper, sticker, or felt cutouts (I prefer the Fun Express Tool Shaped Foam Stickers from Amazon)
- Writing supplies
- Amy Hippo project from Week Four
- Project supplies
- Badge worksheet from Week Three
- Coloring supplies
- Scissors
- Hole punch
- Badge string

Session Plan:

In this session, the counselor will review the client's journal entry, discussing the different skills they shared and utilized during the week. The counselor can ask the client if the person they taught coping skills to knew what coping skills were or if there were any coping skills they regularly practiced. Did the client practice any of these coping skills with this person? The counselor can also see if the client knew to use a coping skill or struggled to decide what to do. Did the coping skills make a difference in the situation? How did the client feel after using the coping skill? Did it make the situation better or worse?

Within the session, the counselor can discuss ways the client can incorporate coping skills into the situations and emotions they bring to the session, or they experienced that week. How would the situation or the client's response change if they used a coping skill then?

In many scenarios, one might not know what skills to use, especially if overwhelmed and experiencing heightened anxiety. It can be tricky to remember coping skills and effectively use them to ease one's emotions. This is where a handy toolbox of coping skills comes into play. This box will serve as the client's toolbox, a place for them to store their coping skills to utilize when things get a bit overwhelming. The counselor and the client can work to list coping skills that have worked or might work to keep in their toolbox. Using small pieces of paper, foam tool stickers, or felt cut into the shape of tools, the client can write a coping skill on each of the pieces to add to their toolbox. In an instance where they are facing big emotions or anxious feelings, they can easily pull a coping tool from the box to complete, working to calm down those feelings. The client can take the box home after the session to keep and use for future situations. With their work on filling their toolbox, the client will be awarded their third badge, the Toolbox badge, to color, cut, and add to their badge collection.

The counselor will continue by introducing ANTs, or Automatic Negative Thoughts, to the client. Additional information regarding the concept of ANTs is available to counselors on the website. These ANTs tend to pop up in our lives naturally, though they can tend to get in the way if they start to infest one's mind with negativity and doubt. With the client, the counselor can discuss the different ANTs that come up in the client's life based on the talk therapy they have done so far, recognizing a pattern and devising ways to understand or cope with these thoughts. By recognizing these thoughts as nothing more than one's brain trying to protect them from trouble or a habit one has formed for themselves, they can understand and cope with the thoughts with more ease and the ability to push them away. These thoughts should not get in the way of the client's life nor hinder their perception of themselves, the world, or the future. The counselor can practice with the client in recognizing the different thoughts they have by going through nine of the more common types of ANTs. With these Automatic Negative Thoughts in mind, the counselor can challenge the client to call out or positively challenge the negative thoughts they have by labeling these thoughts as nothing more than a pesky ANT or by flipping the ANT into a reframed perspective using the CBT Triangle.

ANTs work alongside the CBT Triangle the client learned last week. Automatic Negative Thoughts are an active component in the CBT Triangle being the thoughts that can influence one's feelings, and subsequently their behavior. Working to ease these ANTs can help interrupt the triangle's cycle, creating a healthier mindset for the person. Using instances from the client's talk therapy, the client can make a CBT Triangle using their ANTs to see how they affected their feeling and then behavior.

The client will continue to work on their Amy Hippo project, stuffing their cloth or felt hippo or adding the finishing touches on their crafted hippo. The client will be close to finishing their project and may continue work on their project in the next session.

The weekly mission tasks the client to practice using their toolbox during the week. In their journal, the client will list all the tools they used and when they knew to use them based on the situations and moments they faced that week.

Review:

- Review and discuss the client's journal entry on teaching and using coping skills
- Write coping skills on paper, tool stickers, or felt cut-outs to put in their toolbox, explaining the importance of the toolbox and when to utilize these coping skills
- Award the client with their Toolbox badge
- Introduce and discuss ANTs and how they present themselves in the client's life
- Review the CBT Triangle, explaining and practicing how ANTs work alongside the CBT Triangle
- Continue to work on the client's Amy Hippo project, stuffing or adding touches to their hippo
- For the weekly mission, task the client to practice using their toolbox, listing the tools they used and when they knew to use them

Note to Counselor:

For the toolbox coping skills, the counselor can get creative when it comes to the tools the client will be adding to their box. Paper is always an option, but the counselor can use felt or find or make tool cutouts for the client to use.

With the ANTs lesson, the counselor and client can work to find some of the ANTs hidden throughout the book. These ANTs can be found in Becka's thoughts, as well as by finding the illustrated little ant creatures lingering around her Automatic Negative Thoughts within the storybook pages. With the found ANTs, the client can make a CBT Triangle for Becka, pointing out how her ANT affected her feelings which led to a certain behavior. This can serve as an additional activity for the session.

Week 9
ANTs Badge and Client Role-Play

Summary:

In this session, the counselor will review the client's coping skills entry, discussing the different skills they used and when they knew to use them for the overwhelming moments they faced that week. The counselor and the client will continue their talk therapy session, incorporating the ways the client can utilize their coping skills toolbox in certain situations. Approaching the end of the curriculum, the counselor will bring all the concepts learned throughout the session into the discussion, celebrating and reminding the client of all the new skills they now have in their lives. With all of these concepts, the counselor will task the client to become the "counselor" by role-playing and teaching the different concepts they have learned to the counselor. The client will finish and finalize their Amy Hippo to take home at the end of the curriculum, and color and cut their new badge, the ANTs Triangle badge, to add to their Amy Hippo collar. The client will select their weekly mission to complete.

Objectives:

- Review and recognize the different coping skills the client used and when during the week
- Analyze situations from the session that a coping skill could have benefited and why
- Acknowledge the different skills learned throughout the sessions and utilized in their understanding of their emotions and approach to new situations
- Showcase new skills by effectively role-playing as the counselor teaching the different concepts, and incorporating them into the therapy discussion
- Decide a mission that best fits the client based on the lessons and skills learned through the sessions

Supplies:

- Amy Hippo project from Week Four
- Badges worksheet from Week Three
- Coloring supplies
- Scissors
- Hole punch
- Badge string

Session Plan:

In this session, the counselor will review the client's weekly journal entry, discussing the coping skills they used throughout the week and when they knew to use those coping tools. The counselor can ask the client if they utilized their toolbox and if it made a difference in selecting and practicing those skills in moments of heightened emotions.

The counselor will discuss all the concepts learned so far with the client, prompting the client to recognize how each concept connects. With each skill learned, the client can recognize an increased emotional vocabulary to assist in expressing their individual needs and experiences more effectively. Anxiety, panic, fear, and anger can often be a result of unaddressed emotions, a lack of understanding of one's emotions, and the discomfort these emotions can bring. With each of these lessons, the client can attentively consider the different emotions they might be experiencing and what they mean. They can start to challenge these thoughts and emotions in a confident and empowered way, taking that understanding and control to better manage their emotions, thoughts, and behaviors in the end. Each concept can work together to help the client break down the different situations they face with better clarity and emotional intelligence.

With these new skills under their belt, the counselor will task the client to role-play the skills and "become the counselor" for a moment, teaching each of the key badge concepts to the counselor in a fun and lighthearted way to showcase and celebrate the skills they have achieved. At the end of the demonstration, the counselor can congratulate the client on their success in remembering and internalizing each skill by awarding them their fourth badge, the ANTs badge.

The client will finalize their Amy Hippo project to take home after their graduation day session. They will also color and cut their ANTs badge to add to their Amy Hippo's collar.

The weekly mission is for the client to decide. Based on what they feel is most fitting, the client will choose the mission they want to focus on and complete this week. The counselor can guide the client to focus on the different skills and concepts learned to base their mission around, such as having the client watch another movie, dissecting the scenes and characters similar to their movie night mission, or teaching their friends and family each concept, similar to their pretend counselor session this week. With the guidance of the counselor, the client will choose their mission for the week based on what they want to focus on and achieve. This week's mission can also serve as a make-up day for clients who missed or need to complete a prior weekly mission.

Review:
- Review weekly mission with the client on coping skills
- Incorporate coping skills and the toolbox concept into the therapy session
- Discuss the different concepts learned in the course
- Have the client role-play and "teach" the counselor the five key concepts from the sessions, pretending to be the counselor
- Finalize their Amy Hippo project to take home at the end of the curriculum
- Color and cut the ANTs badge to add to their Amy Hippo collar

Note to Counselor:
When it comes to reviewing the concepts learned throughout the course, it is up to the counselor to go about this activity. It can be a quick review, asking the client questions about each concept, or incorporated into the session, using the concepts to work into the dialogue or use as practice for some situations. If the client has shown an exceptional understanding and use of the concepts, the counselor can move from

this review to focus on the role-playing activity the client will perform to show their content mastery.

If the counselor wants to provide extra guidance for the client in picking their mission, they can make a list of options based on the concepts and prior weekly missions for the client to choose from. This weekly mission can also be a break from the journal entries, allowing the client to work on a mission and share their findings in the next session. If the client is behind in their sessions or weekly missions, this week can act as a make-up week for them, catching up on a mission they failed to do or understand. Either way, this can be a fun week for them to complete an activity they prefer while continuing to practice the concepts and skills learned.

Week 10
Family Session or Flex Day

Summary:

In this session, the counselor will either facilitate a family therapy session, addressing concerns and teaching the parents skills to take home, or use this session to work on any areas where the client requires additional support. The weekly mission tasks the client's parents or guardians to make a list of things they are proud of their child for doing this week based on the lessons and skills learned in the sessions.

Objectives:

- Discuss with parents the concerns and observations gathered within the counseling sessions, moving forward with introducing skills for the parents to apply at home
- Focus on reinforcing concepts in areas where the client needs additional help
- Encourage parents to recognize their child's accomplishments of applying the counseling session tools in their everyday life

Session Plan:

This session can work as either a flex day or a family therapy session. Depending on the availability of the client's parents or guardians, this day can serve as a chance for the counselor to have the parents join the client's session. In the family session, the counselor will address parent and client concerns, discussing the client's progress, the progress of their current treatment plan, and any other topics the counselor deems necessary. This session can also serve as a training experience for the parents, with the counselor teaching the parents emotional skills to take home.

If parents are unavailable, the counselor can use the session to focus on areas the client may need more help or support. The counselor can use this session to reinforce and practice areas where the client might need additional guidance. This session is a chance for the counselor to help move the client along to completing the curriculum and meeting their treatment goals.

This week's mission tasks the client's parents or guardians to list the accomplishments of their child that they are proud of, such as using their toolbox when needed, communicating feelings and needs effectively, and tending to their Amy Hippo when their anxiety starts to peek out. The parents can recognize their child's progress from the first session with all the skills they have learned and the confidence they have developed.

Review:
- Invite parents or guardians to a family therapy session, discussing concerns, questions, and observations and teaching new skills to the parents to use at home
- Or, use the day as a flex day, focusing on areas the client might need more practice and support with
- Assign weekly mission to parents, tasking them to make a list of moments where they were proud of their child that week

Note to Counselor:
For this week, the counselor can decide if a family session is needed or necessary for the client and their counseling plan. However, at times parents or guardians are unavailable or unwilling to participate in their child's treatment. Instead, this session can be used to cover or re-enforce any areas that require additional support. This place in the schedule can act as a spot for counselors to add more weeks into the plan if necessary to ensure sufficient progress towards completing and meeting the client's treatment goals.

Week 11
CBT Case Scenarios and Badge

Summary:

In this session, the counselor will review the client's weekly mission, discussing the list of things their parents or caretakers felt proud of the client for doing. The counselor will role play using CBT case scenarios with the client based on their individual needs and treatment plan, utilizing the Amy Hippo concepts and skills in the different scenarios. The counselor will award the client with their final badge, the CBT Triangle badge, to add to their badge collection. The weekly mission will ask the client to reflect on the moments they used their Amy Hippo skills.

Objectives:

- Participate and act out scenarios focused on the client's counseling session, practicing Amy Hippo concepts to address the situation
- Recognize the Amy Hippo tools and skills the client uses in their everyday lives, actively addressing their Amy Hippo when she wakes up

Supplies:

- Badge worksheet from Week Three
- Coloring supplies
- Scissors
- Hole Punch
- Badge string

Session Plan:

In this session, the counselor will review the client's journal entry, asking the client how they feel about all the things their parents or guardians were proud of them for doing and if they feel proud about their accomplishments.

The counselor will role-play with the client, acting out CBT case scenarios based on the client's individual counseling and treatment plan as they practice the new skills they have adopted over the sessions. The client can apply the communication, processing, and coping skills they have learned to respond more appropriately and with more control when it comes to their emotional reactions. This practice is based on the client's presenting concerns at intake, and considering the discussions shared in the sessions. The Amy Hippo curriculum and lessons can be an additional aspect to the role play with the counselor playing with the different elements to highlight and include in the session based on the client's individual needs and treatment plan.

The counselor will award the client their final badge, the CBT Triangle badge, for their progress on the concept and in this session. The client will color and cut the badge to add to their Amy Hippo collar.

The weekly mission tasks clients to reflect and find moments to be proud of for the use of their new skills in soothing heightened emotional responses that week.

Review:
- Review the client's weekly journal entry created by the client's parent or guardian
- Create situations based on the client's individual counseling sessions and treatment plan to role play and practice using new Amy Hippo skills
- Color and cut the CBT Triangle badge to add to Amy Hippo's collar
- Find moments to be proud of the skills they've learned and used to calm their Amy Hippo

Note to Counselor:
For this session, CBT case scenarios are dependent on the counselor and their techniques for conducting the role-playing practice. The counselor should continue with their practices and techniques for the role-playing activity to best fit the client and their needs. The Amy Hippo curriculum and skills can be modified and adapted to fit within the case scenarios however the counselor feels fit.

Week 12
Graduation Day

Summary:

In this session, the client will recognize their achievements with a graduation party. The counselor will celebrate the client with a treat or special activities, inviting their family or friends to see the client graduate with a whole new set of skills and ways to manage their emotions. The counselor will hold a graduation for the client and their Amy Hippo creation which they will take home at the end of the session.

Objectives:
- Applaud the client on their accomplishments, influencing the client to appreciate all the effort and persistence they put into the curriculum
- Encourage the client to take all the skills they learned and apply them in their lives, recognizing that they are now in charge of their Amy Hippo
- Excite the client to continue strengthening their emotional intelligence

Supplies:
- Graduation party supplies (balloons, streamers, graduation cap, diploma, cake, drinks, etc.)

Session Plan:

In the final session of the curriculum, the counselor will celebrate the client's achievements by throwing a graduation party for the client. The counselor can decorate the space or bring in treats, such as a small cake or drinks. They can bring in paper graduation caps and pretend diplomas for the client and their hippo. The counselor can also invite the client's parents or guardians to the session to further celebrate the client.

The client now has the skills and resources to manage and cope with their emotions and hard situations that come their way. However, hardships do not magically disappear after graduation. There will still be challenging days along the way, but now the client will have the tools to navigate these hard days and difficult situations without holding them back. It's only human to have bad days, but there are awesome days along the way too. The client can now make these harder days a little easier to handle.

At the end of the party, the client will take home the Amy Hippo project they have been working on over the last weeks. Their creation will serve as a reminder for the client of their ability to calm down their Amy Hippo anytime she tries to swoop in when they don't truly need her help. Amy Hippo will always be there, but the client now has the skills to take control in these situations with their Amy Hippo staying around to cheer them on rather than take over.

Review:
- Celebrate the client with a graduation and graduation party
- Have the client take home their Amy Hippo creation

Note to Counselor:
When it comes to the party, the details are completely up to the counselor, considering their resources and capabilities. In the end, the day is to celebrate the client, encouraging them to continue on their journey of understanding and caring for their emotions. Whichever way the counselor can celebrate will make this a special day for the client to remember.

After graduation, the counselor will discuss if the client would benefit from further counseling or if it is requested by the family. Depending on their counseling and treatment plan, the client might have benefitted from the twelve or more weeks of counseling mixed with the Amy Hippo curriculum. The counselor will help the client and family understand when to recognize that a return to counseling for a "tune-up" may be beneficial for the client.

Parents

Our Family's 5-Night Amy Hippo Plan

Date	Adventure	Activity
Night 1	Read Introduction to Amy Hippo Enjoy the Discussion & Journal prompts together Explore the Amy Hippo website together	Color Amy Hippo color page at back of your book (pg. 98)
Night 2	Read Part 1 – Flight Enjoy the Discussion & Journal prompts together	Find the hidden ANTs Review ANTs blog on website Cut & color the ANTs badge (pg. 99)
Night 3	Read Part 2 – Freeze Enjoy the Discussion & Journal prompts together	Did you spot more ANTs? Three Zones Worksheet (pg. 102) Cut & Color Zones badge (pg. 99)
Night 4	Read Part 3 – Fight Enjoy the Discussion & Journal prompts together	Iceberg Worksheet (pg. 101) Cut & Color Iceberg badge (pg. 99)

Night 5	Read Part 4 – Superhero's Toolkit Enjoy the Discussion & Journal prompts together **CELEBRATE!!** It's graduation night! How will you celebrate together?	Complete the Amy Hippo Journaling pages and list as many coping skills as you can think of as a team. Cut & Color coping tools badge (pg. 99) Send Amy Hippo a photo of your completed mission (Adult activity – imperfections blog)

The Amy Hippo curriculum can be utilized at home where parents can use the course to strengthen the entire family's awareness and approach to their emotions, as well as their family members' emotions. This course can help families build effective communication skills and facilitate growth, confidence, and experiences of empowerment for their children.

This course is recommended to be covered and completed over five or six nights within a one-month period. Parents and their children should work on the course together as a team, reading and discussing the story and answering discussion questions.

Night 1
Welcome to the Amy Hippo Course

On the first night, the parent and child will begin by signing their names on the opening page of the book, committing to go on this journey together by completing the fun and beneficial features this book has to offer. As a team, the parent and child will follow the nightly activities and master the skills presented to use after the course is complete. The two will go on to read the first couple of pages of the book, reading the story symbols and glancing at the table of contents. The parent and child will read the "Introduction" where they will meet Amy Hippo and get a hint at the adventure they will be on for the rest of the book. Following the Introduction is the "Amy Asks" section. This section will follow each story, featuring discussion questions and blank answer pages for the parent and child to write or draw their responses. In this "Amy Asks", the parent and child will discuss emotions: what they are, what they feel like, and any stories they have about big or worrying emotions. This discussion is open to drift into other areas and topics, so feel free to let the dialogue lead into its own adventure.

For Night One, the parent can set time aside to finish the section to prevent either the child or parent from feeling rushed or distracted by other obligations. This can be 15-minutes or longer to accomplish everything, whatever fits best for the parent and child that allows enough time to work on the course and fulfill other duties in the day.

Additional activities for this night include exploring the Amy Hippo website to read about the book and to find more activities and resources on emotional skills development. With everything in mind, the parent and child can list things they are hoping to learn as they move through this adventure together.

At the end of the activities, the child will work on personalizing the Amy Hippo coloring page at the back of the book to use in the upcoming nights.

Night 2
Reading and Badge Night: Flight and ANTs

On the second night, the parent and child will go on to read "Part One: Flight" where they will meet Becka James and her superhero Amy Hippo. After the story, the two will find another Amy Asks section to work on and discuss moments of feeling worried, embarrassed, or scared. With the discussions, allow the conversation to drift into other areas and topics that come naturally to the parent or child. All discussion is beneficial, so set forth on any adventure your discussion leads to.

Set aside approximately 30 minutes for tonight's activities to ensure that the child nor the parent feels rushed or distracted by other obligations.

Tonight's activities involve finding the hidden ANTs (Automatic Negative Thoughts) in the story. The parent and the child can flip through the pages together, looking for the different ANTs said or thought. (Hint: look for the illustrated insect ants hidden on pages with ANTs spoken by Becka James) To learn more, visit the Amy Hippo website to read more about ANTs in the blog section.

The goal is for the child to identify the ANTs that occur in tonight's story by the end of the activity. If completed, the parent will award the child their first badge, the ANTs badge, using the Amy Hippo badges for parents PDF found on the website or at the back of this book. The child will color and cut their badge to tape or glue to their Amy Hippo coloring page completed on Night One.

Night 3
Reading and Badge Night: Freeze and Three Zones

On the third night, the parent and child will move on to read "Part Two: Freeze" where they will read about another overwhelming experience Becka James faces. After the story, the two will work on the "Amy Asks" section, focusing on what happened to Becka and moments of feeling frozen in fear. In the discussion, allow the conversation to drift into any avenue it may lead, following the adventure that comes along with it. With this night, set aside approximately 30 minutes to avoid the parent or child from feeling rushed or distracted by other tasks.

In tonight's activity, the parent and child will search for more hidden ANTs in tonight's reading section, having fun by calling out the ANTs when they have been spotted. The parent and child will also learn about the Three Zones that symbolize the three stages of emotional experiences we find ourselves in across varying situations. The first zone, right in the middle of the target, is the **Comfort and Safety Zone** – a zone where we feel comfortable and most at ease, like at home with our feet up or reading in the park. We can relax and recharge in this zone because nothing is challenging or pushing us and we are safe here. This zone is important to help us relax and recharge daily while giving us time to release tensions and let our guard down. Though this stage sounds nice and easy, we are not growing in this zone, so it's important to routinely move beyond the Comfort and Safety Zone. It's also vital that we return to this zone to unwind and embrace feeling secure in our space.

In the next zone, we are moved to a less comfortable space filled with possibilities for progress and discovery. The **Growth and Learning Zone** is the zone where one is ready to engage and be focused on new situations and ideas. Whether in school or social situations, this stage encourages being present and willing to act and interact. This is a stage of personal growth and new experiences, and we can feel anxious in these moments, especially as we're faced with unfamiliar things. It's natural to feel a bit of anxiety and nerves going into a new situation. Yet, in the final zone, the final ring of the target, those early feelings of anxiety and worry reach an unhealthy level and hinder one's progress.

This zone, the **Fear and Anger Zone**, affects the logical side of your brain, turning off rational thought and increasing reliance on emotional responses. This is where Amy Hippo swoops in – the emotional side of your brain is the Amy Hippo control center. From here, Amy Hippo (your brain's **amy**gdala and **hippo**campus) only allows you to react with fight, flight, or freeze. In these moments, it's important to find ways to move back to the middle zone to continue one's growth and positive handling of new situations. This will become achievable with the aid of personal coping skills taught in the upcoming nights of this story.

Once the parent feels that their child has shown an understanding of the basic vocabulary of the Three Zones concept, they can award the child with their next badge, the target-shaped Three Zones badge. The child can color, cut, and tape or glue the badge to their Amy Hippo coloring page at the back of the book.

An optional Three Zones worksheet is available online at www.amyhippo.com or on page 102. To complete the worksheet, help your child color each zone a different color and write one example of an experience that fits each zone. For example, color the Comfort and Safety Zone green and write "napping" or "movie night" in the center most zone. Next, color the Learning and Growth Zone yellow and write "school" or "soccer practice" as the experience. Then, color the Fear and Panic Zone red and write a possible example of "riding a new rollercoaster" or "getting in trouble". Last, allow your child to draw their own facial expressions in the boxes below from the examples they provided for each zone. This will allow them to see how their body and facial expressions change as they move into different zones.

Night 4
Reading and Badge Night: Fight and Anger Iceberg

On the fourth night, the parent and child will read "Part Three: Fight" where they will see Becka's mindset after her soccer game. After the reading, the two will move on to the "Amy Asks" discussion questions, answering questions about Becka's reaction that night at dinner. With the discussion, allow the conversation to drift into other areas to see where the dialogue will take you. Tonight, dedicate a block of time to prevent the parent or child from feeling rushed or distracted by other tasks.

For tonight's activity, the parent and the child will be making an Anger Iceberg for Becka James in this chapter. With an iceberg, we can see a small tip of ice above the surface of the water, but underneath the water is a much larger piece of ice compared to what we see above the water. The tip of the iceberg represents anger that is observable to others around us. In the world of mental health care, anger is often referred to as a "secondary emotion." Anger is seen as commonplace and not often associated with weakness or vulnerability, therefore, it can feel fairly safe for us to display our anger. However, anger is often fueled by primary emotions that frequently provoke sensations of vulnerability when expressed outwardly. Therefore, primary feelings of shame or fear may be expressed with the secondary response of anger as a defense against vulnerability.

For example, you did something embarrassing at school and everyone laughed. Your first reaction visible to others might be anger, but inside you felt embarrassed, ashamed, worthless, or sad. You might not understand why you feel this way or do not want to show that to your friends and peers since allowing increased vulnerability in a public setting can feel intimidating and scary in itself. Place the word "anger" at the tip of the iceberg and "embarrassed," "ashamed," and "sad" in the hidden ice below the surface. This creates a concrete visualization of our experience with anger. Once our experience with anger is expressed as an Anger Iceberg worksheet then we can work to increase our communication skills with a new vocabulary for the family to help check-in with each other. In moments of anger, parents can now suggest or ask their child what could be happening with their Anger Iceberg and work together to better verbalize each experience.

For this Anger Iceberg activity, the two will consider what emotions Becka could have been experiencing at the dinner table that her family couldn't see. Becka's family could clearly see her react with anger. This emotion (anger) will be written at the tip of the iceberg, just above the surface. However, other emotions were hidden below the surface. Together, fill in the bottom of the iceberg, below the surface, with as many other emotions you can think that she might have been feeling but was disguised as anger on the surface. At the end of the activity, the parent will award their child the Anger Iceberg badge to color, cut, and affix to their Amy Hippo coloring page at the back of the book.

There is an Anger Iceberg worksheet available to download and print on the website and also provided on page 101.

Night 5
Reading, Badge, and Celebration Night: Superhero's Toolbox, Coping Skills, and Finishing the Course

On the fifth and final night, the parent and child will read "Part Four: Superhero's Toolbox" where they will learn more about Amy Hippo and different coping skills to calm down big emotions. Together, they will answer the "Amy Asks" discussion questions on the topic of coping skills. With any of the discussions, allow the responses to drift into other areas to see where the dialogue leads and the adventures it creates. For this night, set aside a recommended 60 minutes, to ensure neither the parent nor the child feels rushed or distracted by other obligations.

Tonight's activity tasks the parent and child to complete the Amy Hippo journaling pages in this section and, as a team, list as many coping skills they can think of. Together, the two can discuss coping skills and how they might help in overwhelming situations. After listing and discussing coping skills, the parent will award their child the final badge, the Toolbox badge, to cut and color, adding it to their Amy Hippo coloring page.

A hidden treasure for adults - did you find any imperfections or misspellings in "Part Four"? If so, visit the Amy Hippo website to read more about imperfections and why they can be valuable to each of us.

This night is the final night of the course. The parent and child have a lot to celebrate after five nights of working together and learning new emotional management strategies. That's why tonight is also a celebration night. This truly is a fantastic achievement for you and your child, and celebrating with a special family dinner, extra time together, or a small treat can help make the moment feel even more significant and help the skills learned last a lifetime for your family.

Once all four badges are earned and the child's Amy Hippo is complete, take a photo to celebrate the wonderful achievement. Consider sharing a photo of your child's finished coloring sheet and badges with Amy Hippo herself on the website.

Note to Parents

The skills learned and achieved throughout the course can benefit your child in the many years to come, aiding in building a vocabulary to discuss big feelings within the safety and comfort of your family and home. These are impressive skills for any child to learn at any age. If you are experiencing behavioral challenges or have concerns for your child's overall mental health, please follow-up with a local counselor for extra assistance to help turn these Amy Hippo skills into a behavioral support plan for your family. The website, www.psychologytoday.com is a terrific resource to search for local counselors, filtering results to find counselors available near you and who accept your insurance.

Supplementary Materials

- Amy Hippo Coloring Sheet
- Badges
- Anger Iceberg Worksheet
- Three Zones Worksheet
- ANTs flashcards

Color your own Amy Hippo

Amy Hippo
Badges
(Teachers & Parents)

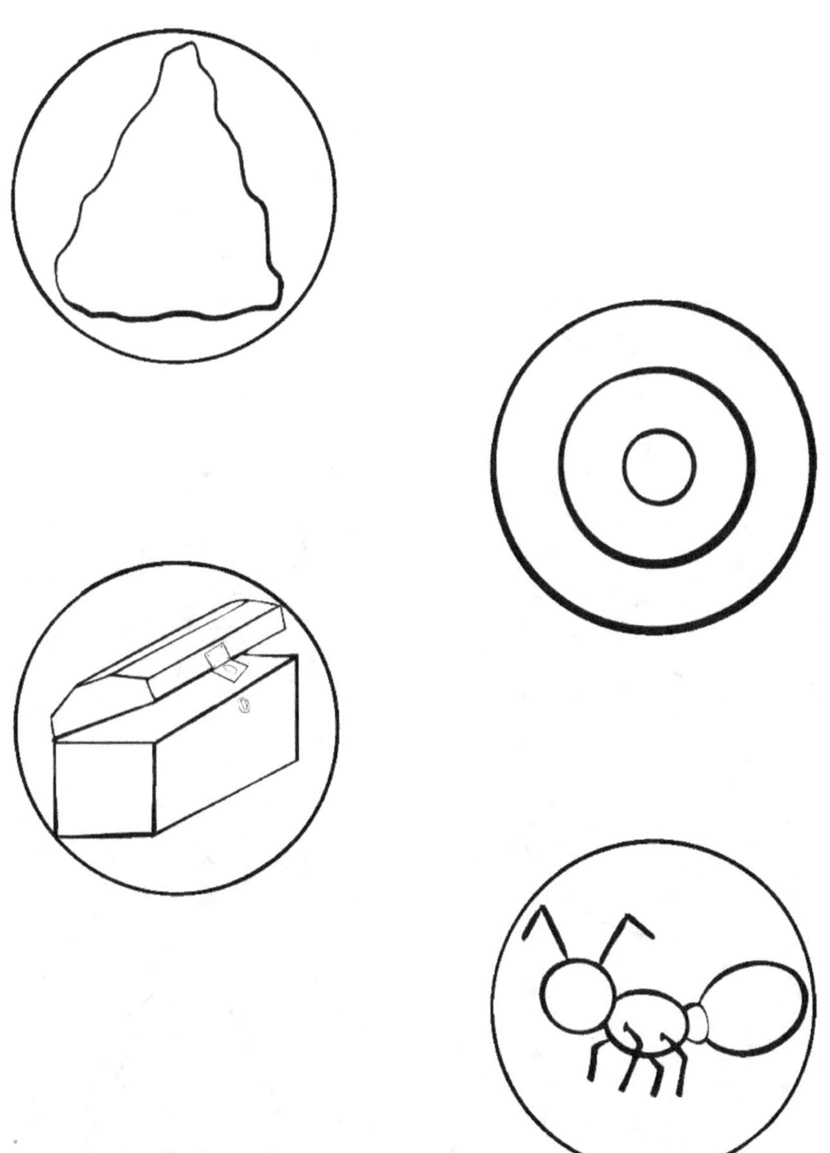

Amy Hippo
Badges

(Counselors)

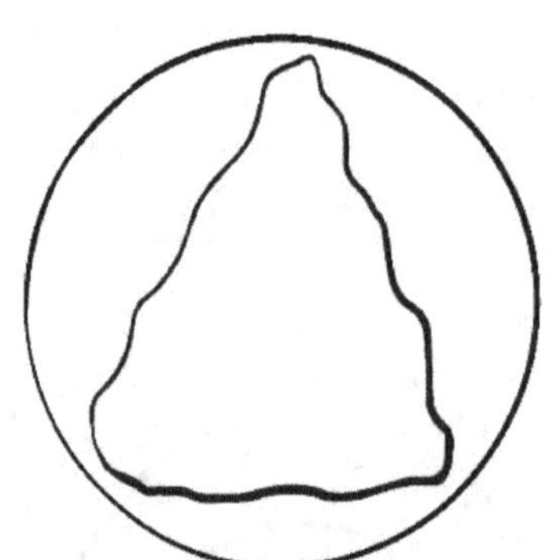

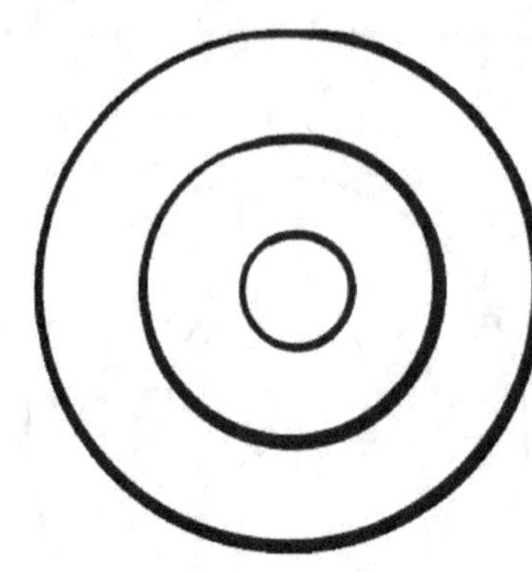

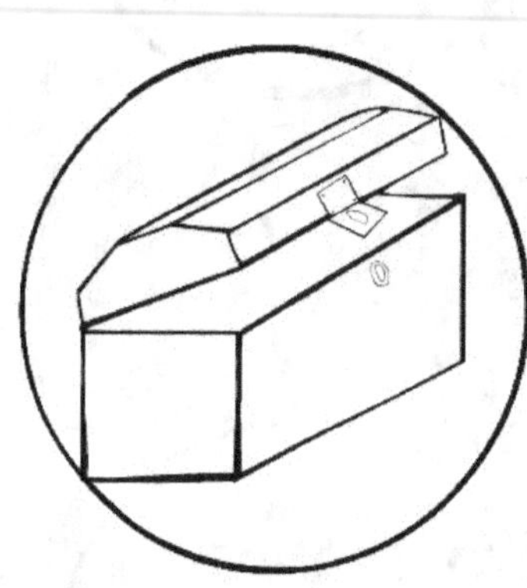

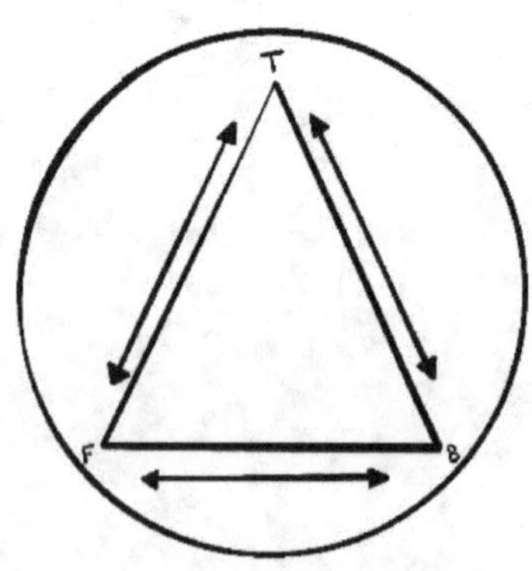

My 3 Zones

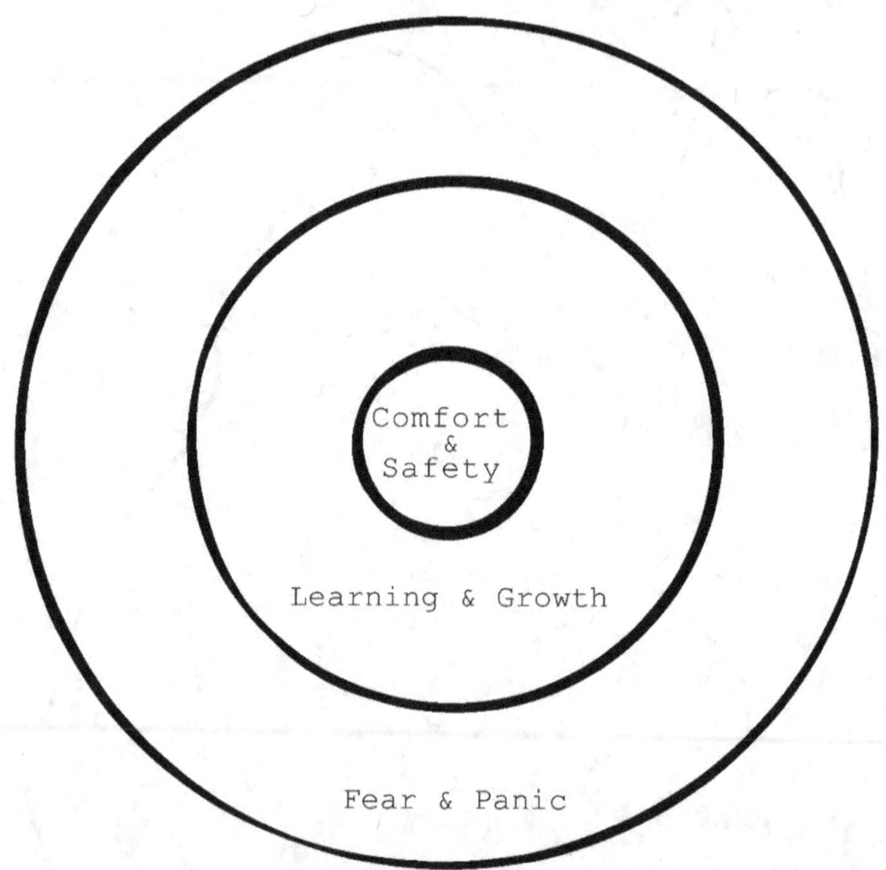

Draw your face below. How would you look in each
of the zones?

Black & White Thinking
(All or Nothing)

Focusing on the Negative

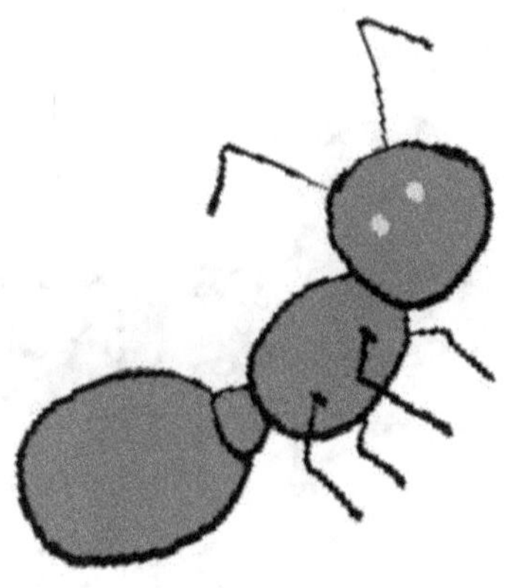

Fortune Telling

Mind Reading

Thinking with
Your Feelings

Ruled by "Shoulds"

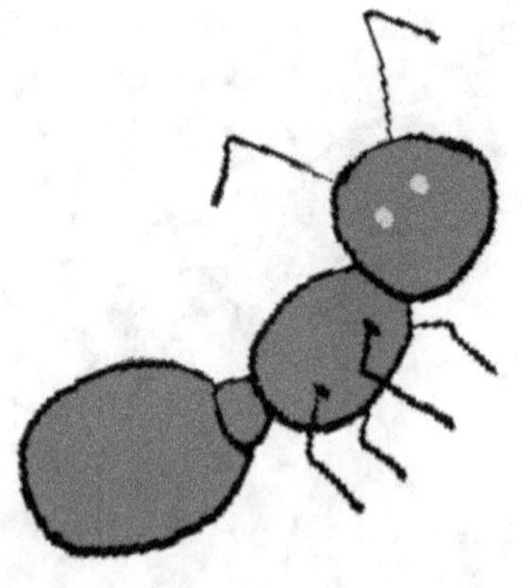

Labeling

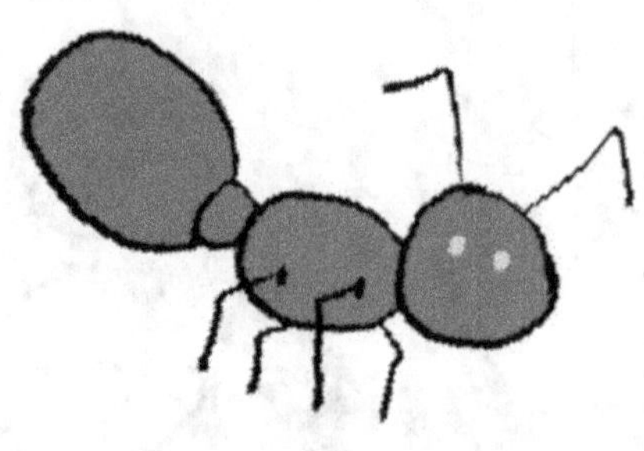

Personalizing

Blaming

Catastrophizing

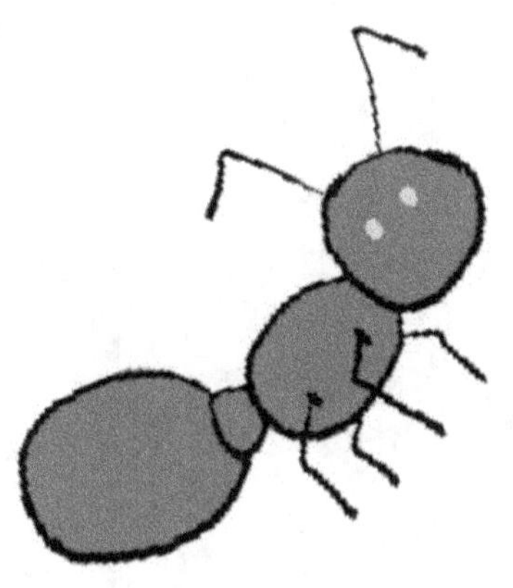

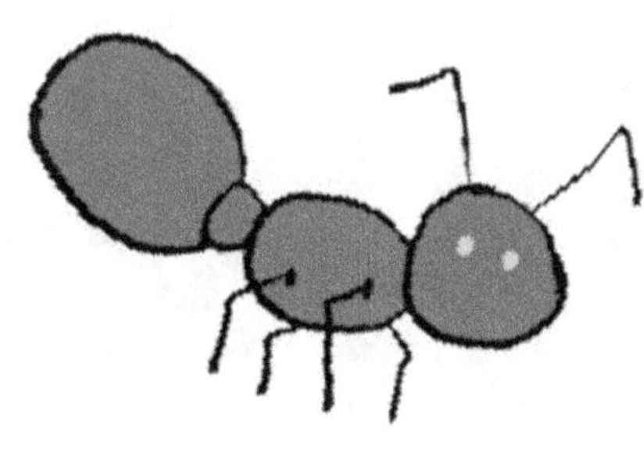